STUDENTS LEAD NOW

THE ULTIMATE GUIDE TO STUDENT LEADERSHIP

WRITTEN BY STUDENT LEADERS FOR STUDENT LEADERS

ROHULLAH LATIF

DANIEL CLARK

TAYLOR HERREN

KAREEM AREF

JUDITH MARTINEZ

Editor/Author: Rohullah Latif | Daniel Clark
Authors: Taylor Herren | Kareem Aref | Judith Martinez
Cover Design by: Jonathon Kwok

A special "thank you" to Dalia El Hindawy Aref and
Dr. Wm. Gregory Sawyer for providing us support along the
way.

ISBN-13: 978-1530674626

ISBN-10: 153067462X

CONTENTS

ACKNOWLEDGMENTS

This book would have not been possible without the support that we, as student leaders received from our friends and mentors during our elected terms. It has been an incredible honor serving our constituents as student leaders on our campuses. We truly believe that student leadership has changed our lives forever and for the better and as such, we believe that it too, will change yours.

LEAD ON!

EDITORS | AUTHORS

Rohullah Latif is a native of Afghanistan and came to the U.S right before 911 without speaking a word of English. Rohullah Latif served as the Student Body President of California State University of Fullerton 2013-2014. He served one of the largest universities with a population of over 38,000 students, and managed a budget of over $15 million. Since graduation, Rohullah has launched 2 companies, one of which he sold, works full time as a Mechanical Engineer in the Medical Device industry, and is pursuing his Masters Degree in Biomedical Engineering at The Johns Hopkins University. In 2015, he accepted the Hall of Fame honor from CSUF on behalf of all student leaders that came before him at California State University, Fullerton. He owes all of his success to the lessons he learned as a student leader, and wishes to pass down that knowledge to future generations. Rohullah, along with Daniel, was the first to develop the writing team and bring this book, in its entirety, to fruition.

Daniel Clark served as both President and Vice President of Legislative Affairs for one of the largest statewide student organizations, the California State Student Association. CSSA is a 501(c)(3) non-profit dedicated to maintaining and enhancing access to an affordable and quality public higher education for the people of California. CSSA represents over 460,000 students at 23 different campuses in the California State University (CSU) system. Daniel represented students before the CSU Chancellor's Office, campus officials, and state and federal government leaders. Prior to his work in the CSU, Daniel was a Region V Senator for the Student Senate for California Community Colleges, an organization that represents over 2.4 million community college students. There, he organized The March in March as well as founded the Latino Caucus and Veterans Caucus organizations that advocated exclusively for Latinos and Veterans. Daniel is a graduate of both Fresno City College and California State University, Fresno. He is currently pursuing his Masters Degree in Education at the University of the Pacific

AUTHORS

An instigator at heart, philosopher by trade, Judith is a recent grad out to make a difference in the world. A proud millennial, Judith is a SoCal native, NorCal educated and a social entrepreneur. Studying Pre-law, Business, and Communications in the heart of Silicon Valley, Judith was Student Body President at one of the nation's top private schools, Santa Clara University. Since graduating, she has founded InHerShoes, a registered 501(c)(3) non-profit committed to catalyzing courage for young girls and women around the world to live lives of empowerment, exploration, and possibility. With over 12 years of student leadership and advocacy experience within her communities and higher education, Judith is committed to shifting the conversation for young people from "What can I do?" to "Who can I be?" - taking student leadership outside of formal education into life. Judith has worked with global organizations such as Ashoka: Innovators for the Public, world-class leaders such as Leon Panetta, and shares her voice on behalf of youth around the world at the Youth Assembly, United Nations.

Kareem Aref has been a student advocate since graduating High School. As a first year at the University of California Riverside, Kareem began working with the office of External Affairs. He Co-Founded the California Union of College and University Students, an initiative that sought to unite over 3 million students in the state of California. In 2012 as the Associated Students Legislative Affairs Director, Kareem launched what would become one of the strongest student lobby presences in the nation. During this same time, Kareem Served as the Secretary Finance officer for the University of California Student Association (UCSA) where he managed the organizations documents, budget and transitioned the organization to a 501(c)(3). The following year as Vice President of External Affairs representing UCR on the UCSA board of directors, Kareem was nominated and elected President of the statewide student association. In this capacity Kareem represented over 240,000 students statewide on issues of Accessibility, Affordability, Quality of the university and social justice. Kareem's work in student advocacy was the single most transformative experience of his life and continues to mentor and work with students and higher education to this day.

Taylor Herren is currently a graduate student at the California State University (CSU), Chico where she studies Sustainable Agriculture and Environmental Policy. She has been involved as a student leader and as an activist on her campus as well as an advocate for the scientific community and higher education. She was twice elected President of CSU, Chico's Associated Students, where she served as the official voice of her peers and the CEO of a $20-million corporation from 2013-2015. Taylor continued her student leadership journey into 2015 after being elected to represent nearly half-a-million California State University students as President of the California State Student Association. In addition to her work on the West Coast, she regularly travels to Washington, DC and lobbies support for STEM education and scientific research through organizations like National Campus Leadership Council and the American Institute of Biological Sciences. Her goal is to become an established leader in both the agriculture industry and the public policy sector who devotes her career to bridging gaps between policy makers, scientists, and agriculturists in the interest of creating equitable, healthy and resilient future generations.

Lead on!
~ Doc

MENTOR

Dr. Wm. Gregory Sawyer, a native of Columbus, Ohio, is the founding Vice President for Student Affairs at California State University Channel Islands (CI). Dr. Sawyer earned his Ph.D. in Higher Education Administration and was the founding Dean of Students and Chief Student Affairs Officer at Florida Gulf Coast University and the former Dean of Students at the University of North Texas. He has been recognized by the National Association of Student Personnel Administrators (NASPA) as a Pillar of the Profession (2016), and the NASPA Region VI Scott Goodnight Award for outstanding performance as a Vice President for Student Affairs (2013); and by the American College Personnel Association (ACPA) for Excellence in Practice (2016), as a Diamond Awardee (2015) and Senior Practitioner of the Year (2007). Sawyer was also named the Most Distinguished Black Citizen by the Ventura County NAACP, Channel Islands Outstanding Administrator of the Year (2005), and he was selected out of 46,000 faculty and staff by the Trustees and Chancellor of the California State University (CSU) system for the Wang Family Excellence Award as the Outstanding Administrator of the Year (2008). In 2013, California Governor Jerry Brown, appointed Sawyer to the California Student Aid Commission (CSAC) as the CSU System Commissioner.

VII

LATIF| CLARK| HERREN| AREF| MARTINEZ

CONTRIBUTORS

JOURDAN HILAIRE, M. ED | FORMER PRESIDENT OF A.P.A.C.
CALIFORNIA STATE UNIVERSITY, FULLERTON

KELSEY BREWER | STUDENT TRUSTEE
BOARD OF TRUSTEES, CALIFORNIA STATE UNIVERSITY

ZOE JIMENEZ | FORMER RESIDENT ASSISTANT
UNIVERSITY OF NOTRE DAME

MARIAM SALAMEH | FORMER STUDENT BODY PRESIDENT
CALIFORNIA STATE UNIVERSITY, STANISLAUS

STUDENTS LEAD NOW

DANNY O' DONOVAN | STUDENT UNION PRESIDENT
CORK INSTITUTE OF TECHNOLOGY, IRELAND

KATY JOHNSON | STUDENT BODY VICE PRESIDENT
CALIFORNIA STATE UNIVERSITY, FULLERTON

NICHOLAS AYALA | FORMER STUDENT BODY PRESIDENT
SAN JOSE STATE UNIVERSITY

HARPREET BATH | FORMER STUDENT BODY PRESIDENT
CALIFORNIA STATE UNIVERSITY, FULLERTON

JONNY LEGGETT | FORMER STUDENT BODY VICE PRESIDENT
CALIFORNIA STATE UNIVERSITY, FULLERTON

LATIF| CLARK| HERREN| AREF| MARTINEZ

KEYRA GALVANCO | CHAIR OF THE YOUTH EMPOWERMENT PROGRAM
SANTA CLARA UNIVERSITY

NAYIRI BAGHDASSARIAN | FORMER STUDENT BODY VICE PRESIDENT
CALIFORNIA STATE UNIVERSITY, LONGBEACH

FILIPE CARVALHO | MEMBER OF THE BOARD OF DIRECTORS
UNITED STATES STUDENT ASSOCIATION

LOURDES AMENTE | STUDENT BODY PRESIDENT
SAN JOSE STATE UNIVERSITY

TALAR ALEXANIAN | FORMER STUDENT TRUSTEE
BOARD OF TRUSTEES, CALIFORNIA STATE UNIVERSITY

FORWARD

DR. WM. GREGORY SAWYER, PHD | FOUNDING VICE PRESIDENT FOR
STUDENT AFFIARS
CSU CHANNEL ISLANDS

For thousands of years, humans have been enthralled, mystified and sometimes even paralyzed with the concept of leadership and leaders. From cave dwellers to Emperors, from Chiefs to Presidents, the strength and commanding presence of leaders has always intrigued the masses. There have been tens of thousands of books written world-wide on the subject of leadership; who has it, how did they get it and of course, how do they keep it. In the modern age of technology, hundreds of consultants have created on-line seminars to train and test our transferable leadership skills. On any day, in a major hotel in America, a multi-millionaire will pass on their unequivocal leadership skills in a five-hour seminar. What I find so fascinating about leadership and leading is that there truly are transferable skills that do apply to multiple settings and a variety of venues.

A couple of years ago, while hosting a California State Student Association (CSSA) meeting on my campus of California State University Channel Islands (CI), I had the distinct opportunity to meet one of those unique leaders who indeed possessed the ability to not only understand the concept of leadership but more importantly, how to employ it as part of his personal and professional acumen. Rohullah Latif, then the Student Body President at California State University Fullerton, captured my interest as we passionately discussed views on student leadership. More importantly how to communicate these transferable skills to other students as they began to take on their newly elected roles on their respective campuses.

Of no surprise, Mr. Latif had already vetted this concept with Mr. Daniel Clark (former California State Student Association President and co-author of this book) as well as other student leaders (Mr. Aref, Ms. Martinez, Ms. Herren) throughout California and the nation. Mr. Latif & Mr. Clark were truly thinking like leaders that they are; they were visioning for a better and more sustainable future for continuing campus student leaders rather than the "here and now" platform. It was at that point I remember suggesting that they put these ideas on paper. I then offered my assistance to them in any form they should need. And this is how this incredible book which is student inspired, student written, and student focused systematically and intentionally unfolded.

The Reverend Dr. Martin Luther King, Jr. once said that "Life's most persistent and urgent question is, what are you doing for others?" I believe that the authors of this book have poignantly answered this persistent and urgent question. They have penned an experiential document that provides a bird's eye view of their past experience, their successes as well as their challenges. Through their past experiences as student leaders on campus that they could "pay-forward" this knowledge to newly elected or selected student leaders so they would not have to start from scratch.

I am proud to be associated with forward thinking and visionary leaders like the authors of this book; they are bringing new meaning to a very old concept. Enjoy turning the pages of this insightful and creative blueprint of student leadership from an experiential point of view.

1. INTRODUCTION

ROHULLAH LATIF | FORMER STUDENT BODY PRESIDENT
CSU FULLERTON

My heart is pounding. My legs are shaking. The sun's rays reflect off my glasses. I cannot hear myself think. The noise around me is deafening. Forty thousand people in a huge auditorium are anxiously waiting for the ceremony to start. Surrounded by the university's top administrators, I stood alone on the platform as the only student. Suddenly, my name is called and I walk towards the podium, grab the microphone, and start speaking. After a minute or so, it began to settle in. I looked out and saw my family sitting in the front row; my mother with loving tears in her eyes and my fellow graduates smiling and cheering me on. I realized that my term as Student Body President was coming to an end, and I was graduating. I had earned my undergraduate degree; but more importantly, I was leaving a legacy at my university.

If you have the privilege of serving your campus as a student leader, these opportunities will present themselves to you. One of my favorite mentors once told me, "Anything that you do, whether it is school work, volunteering, or working, give it all you've got." After all, you are in school to graduate and become as successful as possible in your respective professional career. Your student leadership position is temporary; take what you can from it and leave an everlasting legacy. Treat every single opportunity as if it was your last. Doing so will allow you to overcome any obstacle in your student leadership journey.

I was elected Student Body President at California State University, Fullerton in May of 2013. I had won my election, but what next? It had been almost 4 weeks of campaigning and I had lost ten pounds from the stress. I received no training from my predecessor and I felt in over my head. I started conducting research online on how to be a president. I went from being an average student to overseeing an organization with an operating budget of $15 million while representing 38,000 students. Can you guess how many results came up when I searched? A whopping **zero**….. and that is exactly why this book exists!

Politics, long nights, and thankless days. These are all things that you may deal with as a student leader. But at the end of the day, when the work is done and the emails have been sent, when the meeting adjourns and the door closes, you will realize the experience you have gained and the relationships you have built have changed your life. It will not be easy; in fact, it will often be the most trying thing you will have ever dealt with. Some will not make it, but if you do, you will have emerged as an unstoppable force.

This book is meant to be an introduction for students interested in student leadership and a guide for newly elected or appointed student leaders. This book is to inform everyone about the life of a student leader, the possible obstacles they have to overcome on a daily basis, and how to become successful in their respective position.

Imagine if student leaders could learn about some of these challenges and better prepare themselves before their term. During my Presidency, I began jotting down ideas and experiences to one day be able to share it with other student leaders.

That dream became a reality once I met some exceptionally talented leaders who shared the same vision as I did. Together, we developed a book about the life of a student leader drawn from personal examples and experiences. We understand that student leaderships resonate differently with each person. Which is why we have integrated 5 different student leaderships styles in 1 book to ensure the readers are receiving a variety of different perspectives.

Each chapter is then followed by a contribution from another student leader to further provide a thorough understanding of the chapter. We are a team of former student leaders and through this book, offer to you, our collective knowledge and experience, so that you too can leave an everlasting legacy on your campus

2. EDUCATIONAL SYSTEMS AND THE ROLE OF A STUDENT LEADER
ROHULLAH LATIF | STUDENT BODY PRESIDENT
CSU FULLERTON

"We study the past to understand the present; we understand the present to guide the future."

– William Lund

History always tends to repeat itself in some shape, way, or form, and student governments are no exception. Looking to the organization's past and gaining a firm foundation to ground yourself will help you understand the problems you could potentially face in the future. Most issues that come up during your term have most likely been addressed previously. You cannot truly begin to appreciate where you are going if you do not know where you've been.

Student activism, student government, and the student voice are an integral part of a university and have been around as long as colleges and universities themselves. University policy has been revolutionized by the voices of the students who have refused to accept the status quo and sought out changes within their university. The student "voice" and the vision of its leaders differs from campus to campus and era to era; but regardless of the focus or vision, there is no denying the power that students have or the change they can accomplish when united. It all starts with three basic questions:

- Why are you doing this?
- Why is student leadership important to you?
- Why is the student voice important to you?

Not only must you ask these questions at the beginning, you need to continuously be raising the same questions throughout your journey as a student leader. Adam Fletcher, a youth education advocate, said it best during a speech explaining how essential it is that the student voice is heard.

"It is not enough to simply listen to student voices. Educators have an ethical imperative to do something for students, and that is why meaningful student involvement is vital to school improvement."

A university cannot exist without students, yet more often than not, the student voice is not as loud as it should be. We have seen that when students are heard, the university is able to provide an educational experience that is truly reflective of their needs and experiences. Student groups are designed to amplify this voice and create positive change for students and ensure that university administration is putting students at the forefront of every decision-making discussion on campus.

The voice of a student leader needs to reach far beyond the collegiate level and be a force in all levels of government. Your voices and stories can drive policymakers to draft effective policies that impact all aspects of education. Decision makers can be disconnected to the needs of today's students, and it is up to the student leaders to inform them of pressing issues. If students do not take part in the policy making process, we run the risk of allowing policy to detrimentally affect our educational experience. In order for the student voice to truly be heard, it has to come directly from you; as student leaders you are the primary conduit to convey the needs of students.

You must turn your access into their microphone.
Understanding the confines of the system in which your
college falls under, is essential to successfully navigating
the political process.

Components on a Macro & Micro Level

The macro level delves into the bigger picture, the
government, the collective higher education system, and
the larger forces at play in the system. The micro level
consists of the landscape of your campus. Your efficacy is
directly proportional to your ability to use the intricacies
to your advantage. Being a successful student leader
means understanding the current system you will have to
navigate. Student leaders must come to understand all
levels of governance, sources of funding, and have a
complete understanding of the institutional history.
Remember, you cannot build a puzzle if you do not have
all the pieces.

Understanding the Macro Level

Governing Structure

Understanding shared governance at the macro level
means knowing who the decision-makers are outside of
campus and what role they have with respect to your
school. This includes system wide boards as well as the
local, state, and federal governments. You must look at
your campus from a macro level and recognize how it fits
into the overall institutional system of your college or
state.

Funding

Understanding how your college is funded and who
makes decisions affecting your schools funding, can help
you set your agenda for the year. Public universities are

typically funded through public tax dollars. This means advocating to policy makers and ensuring they hear the student voice needs to be part of your agenda. In contrast, private schools must generate their own funding, which usually comes from a variety of sources: tuition; private grants; and fundraising. These are some questions to ask yourself to gain a better understanding of how your campus is funded:

- Does your campus receive money from the state or federal government entity? If so, how much and what is it being used for?
- How does state and federal financial aid directly impact the grants and loans your students receive?
- If you come from a private school, how is your campus funded? Private school funding is different from public school funding.

Understanding the System at a Micro Level

Governing Structure
You must not only understand the formalized systems of power that exist (chancellors, presidents, etc.), but also the ways in which informal power and influence come into play. Here, personalities and politics can play a large role as student demographics, views of administration, and decisions of the campus directly affect each person involved differently. The trick is to understand the flow of power and use that to influence the right people to support your cause.

Funding
Campuses vary in the resources they offer to students. Even the best equipped university is not perfect.

Knowing how your campus collects and allocates funds is useful when classes are getting cut or students do not have the resources they need to be successful. Funding can help drive your advocacy efforts and give you the direction you need to channel your work. In addition to understanding the source of your university's income, it can also be useful to know how money is allocated. Are there areas on your campus that are in need of additional revenue? Are there projects that could be accomplished with extra funds? Understanding the university's complex budget can be overwhelming and confusing for students.

By engaging with the administration, students can gain a greater understanding of how the resources flow. For instance, students were concerned about the increased cost of parking permits at a nearby campus. The purpose behind the increase was to meet the demand for parking by building another parking structure. Unaware of the real reason, students began protesting out of frustration. This could have been mitigated and even avoided if students were properly educated on the university budget. If the appropriate relationship exists, it can be helpful to have the university financial officer present the university budget to your student organization. If you do not have that connection, you can try to build it. The university administration will be more than happy to provide you the tools you need to understand the university better and avoid confusion. This allows for a better understanding of the overall financial structure of the university, and helps alleviate concerns. Ask yourself the following questions regarding your school budget.

- Where does the funding for your university come from (what percentage comes from the state, tuition, grants, etc.)
- How is the budget broken down?
- What is the process for building, approving, and distributing the funds?
- How does your college fund itself and how is money distributed?
- How large is your budget?
- Who are the right people to go to for these answers?

History

Every university system is guided by core values and institutional priorities that are derived from its history. These values encompass everything from its origins to its daily administrative discussions. Every situation that you find yourself in typically has been preceded by many conversations and events. Your ability to make real progress on an issue lies in having a full understanding of the back-story and previous work. Understanding the institutional identity of your campus will help level the playing field during important discussions. Take for example, the goal of installing solar panels on a student union to provide clean energy for the campus.

In pursuing this goal, research is conducted, discussions take place, and after 2 months of work, Fatima finds out that 5 years earlier, the same initiative was undertaken, but could not be completed due to the building structure and the surrounding trees. If Fatima had been aware of the history, she would not have wasted 2 months of hard work and could have instead created a new action plan with the work of the past in mind. In order to avoid being in the same situation as Fatima ask yourself the following questions to gain a better understanding of your university:

- Why was the school founded?
- What has the leadership team accomplished? Both from the university administrator and student leader side.
- What previous projects have they worked on?
- Have their decisions had a positive or negative impact on different groups and organizations?

Different Forms of Student Governments

Student governments come in all shapes and sizes and exist in both public and private schools. They can be referred to as Senates, Associations, or Student Unions. Regardless of the name one thing is certain, you should understand the following elements of student governments in order to understand how to best utilize your own assets.

Association Size

Student governments vary in size depending on the campus and structure. Some student governments like Fresno State University only represent students on their own campus. Other student governments like Florida Atlantic University have multiple campuses and as such have multiple student governments.

The United States Student Association represents millions of students from across the US and operates similar to other lobby groups where individuals buy into their services. The size of the association is key to understanding the amount of influence your organization can have.

Operational Structure

College campuses have various levels of autonomy and operational abilities. Budgets can range from a couple thousand dollars to millions. Organizational structure can be understood as falling into one of two broad categories: direct elections and parliamentary elections. Direct election consists of electing individuals directly to their positions while the latter allows for those elected to decide their own executive team.

Direct election is an executive model. Under this model, student governments have a President and several Vice Presidents each specializing in a distinct area (Vice President of Finance, External Affairs, etc). This will be accompanied by some form of general representation typically a Board of Directors or another board for checks and balance. This board usually meets in committees internally as well as externally depending on its involvement on campus.

Other student government groups mimic The US government, where they are separated into different branches, each having their own checks and balance. Some student governments may also have separate student organizations. One for undergraduate and another for graduate students which do not interact with one another when it comes to policy development or working with the campus.

The University of California, Davis, for example, has student government groups for their undergraduate and graduate students. These types of student governments usually have multi-branch systems with a legislative body (a senate or board), executive (president and vice presidents) and a judicial council, who typically regulate the legality of resolutions or actions taken during the year based on the association's constitution.

KEY CONCEPTS

1. Universities and colleges are designed to serve students and, as such, the student voice has a place in every discussion impacting the educational experience. Be confident in that idea and bold in asserting yourself in those discussions.

2. When setting and pursuing goals, always ask yourself, "why are you doing whatever it is you are doing?" Continuously asking this will ensure you are making thoughtful and grounded decisions.

3. On the macro level, the governing structure, funding, and history of the larger systems and policies at play will allow you to understand how the external influences impact the students you represent directly.

4. On a micro level, understanding the governing structure, funding, and history of your institution will allow you to be effective in making change directly on campus.

5. Understanding the past and the issues previous student government administrations faced is crucial to understanding how the current issues and challenges on your campus came to be.

6. Although there are many student governments, their purpose remains the same: to be the voice of the student body and to create positive change on their behalf.

MY REFLECTION

NAYIRI BAGHDASSARIAN | FORMER STUDENT BODY VICE
PRESIDENT
CALIFORNIA STATE UNIVERSITY, LONG BEACH

I was a three-term Student Body Vice President, which some people might say is impressive. Others might question why after one term I did not run for president. So let me add some context: I was a three-term student body Vice President serving two terms while attending Citrus College Community College in Glendora, CA and one term at California State University, Long Beach (CSULB). I am too big of a parliamentary procedure aficionado to have been a Student Body President.

I have never been afraid to ask questions and find answers. What I noticed early on in my collegiate career was that, although I was surrounded by thousands of hard working students, a great number of them did not know about any of the resources the school had available for them. That really bothered me. I saw a lot of potential in my fellow peers and there was no reason why their path to success had to be any harder than it already was. Going for that degree is not easy and I wanted students to know that someone close by had their back. So that is what fueled me to run for the Vice President position.

I began my career as the Student Body Vice President for my local community college. If you thought a traditional 4-year university had a diverse population, you need to visit a community college. There are students who, like me at the time, just graduated from high school. There were those who went back to school after twenty years because they either got laid off or needed a refresher course to move up in their career.

There are also students who had been attending school since the 1960's because they simply could. Still in my teens, my job was to make sure that my community college was tending to the needs of those students and everyone in between. After two years at Citrus College, I graduated and transferred to CSULB. I immediately joined their student governing body, Associated Students, Inc. (ASI). This was a whole different ball game. ASI is a 501(c)(3) non-profit and acts as both a student government and its own multi-million-dollar corporation. I was the Vice President and the Chair of the Board of Directors. I ran and promised the same thing I promised during my time at Citrus College; capitalizing on the fact that CSULB was known as a commuter school. In my eyes, that meant that it was easier for students to access what they wanted and needed because they were either always on campus or close by. Similar to my experience at Citrus Community College, I realized that many students were not aware of resources available to them. They did not know they had a Student Success Center available to them, they did not know what services the Health Center provided, and more often than not they believed that the role of ASI was the same as the role of a high school ASB.

From my experience, the two student governments had the same objective: to ensure that their students were well equipped with tools to help them survive and succeed college. However, their methods are very different. Community college students are usually too preoccupied about transferring, getting another job, or holding onto the one they have to even know to ask for help to make their college experience easier.

University students generally have a more academic focus with the addition of being involved with a club on campus.

I joined student government because sometimes classes do not have enough left-handed desks. I joined student government because I know how great it is to know that I have unlimited free access to tutors, and why having a DSS office and an EOPS office are gifts from above. I joined because I had friends who were too intimidated by the word "Administration" written on a building to go inside to ask for help. I ran for Vice President because I am a policy nerd and one of my biggest strengths is making sure that school administrators and politicians remember that schools were made to serve students and to help people become productive members of society. That's why I was a three-term student body Vice President.

3. THE ART OF ADVOCACY
KAREEM AREF | PRESIDENT
UNIVERSITY OF CALIFORNIA STUDENT ASSOCIATION

The previous chapter described a seemingly never-ending list of variables that make the role of student leaders so unique from one another. On your campus, the primary function of student leaders may best be described using terms like representative, decision-maker, negotiator, and even public figures. Regardless of their role or title, student leaders have one thing in common: they are all advocates.

At the most basic level, no matter who you are or what position you hold, your most fundamental duty is to do something. As a student leader, you have a responsibility to your constituents to take on the issues that are most important to them. In order to do this, you must engage in an age old tradition of activism through advocacy.

Different Forms of Advocacy
"Students united will never be divided!" shouted 10,000 students as they marched towards the capitol building in California. Every segment of public higher education was represented as students gathered to fight against growing tuition and state divestment from education. The shouts echoed through the streets, as the officers on horseback watched from afar. As the capitol steps grew near the students gathered in protest.

"Whose university!?
Our university!
When they say cut back, we say fight back!"

As the protest grew louder and louder, one could have wondered, where were the legislators? In fact, small groups of students were meeting with legislators in person to convey the importance of prioritizing education in California and months later a tuition freeze was announced. This example showcases two types of advocacy that exist within student leadership; radicalism and diplomacy.

Radicalism

The radical approach is often taken when the system is failing and must be altered. Certain institutions of power are beyond repair and attempting to work through the system is futile. The sad truth is that some systems of power are not designed to do what is best but what is most profitable. In a nutshell, radicalism is often seen when a system gives no other option. Radicalism can be explained as breaking down the door and requires a high level of organization among your constituency. Throughout history, we have seen this method used successfully. The civil rights movement saw this method used in various sit-ins and peaceful protests.

More recently the group *99Rise* has made huge waves in California by taking a small group on a 400-mile march from Los Angeles to Sacramento. The strength came from the dedication of the individuals involved. A sit in with 20 people can be more effective than a riot if executed correctly. The disruption causes and often forces people to understand or at least show concern regarding your cause. While discussions with legislators can be effective, a huge statement can be made with a large march.

As mentioned at the opening of this chapter, in 2011 the universities and colleges of California united for what was coined as the March in March. The energy and power that comes with that many individuals united for a cause can serve as a huge political wake up call, especially for the politicians who depend on the student votes.

Uniting a student constituency in this way is essential for advocating effectively. The most effective speaker alone can never be as loud as hundreds of thousands of people. When a system is failing, it is important to display legitimacy by showing that your cause is supported by many. The 2012 election in California saw an increase in voter turnout in which students between the ages of 18-24 were a majority of the electoral vote. In the wake of this event, politicians began to pay attention to the students of California. Innovative legislations were proposed and for several years, tuition freezes were granted, and students began to be heard. It is important to realize that while marches, protests, rallies and actions can be immensely effective to make a movement known, they are not necessarily enough to make your voice heard. In order to be effective one must understand that there is a time to be seen and a time to be heard. This leads to the second form of advocacy, diplomacy.

Diplomacy
Diplomacy can be defined as, "a skill in handling affairs without arousing hostility." I would like to amend this definition for the purposes of this discussion to a form of advocacy that requires one to work through the system to effect the desired changes in that system.

While radicalism requires one to advocate from outside, diplomacy works through the current institutions of power. With diplomacy, it is more important to present your points clearly and gain buy-in.

Student leadership is temporary and by the time you adjust to your position, it is time for you to pass the torch on to another leader. In addition, student leaders are facing a large learning curve that comes from working with senior university administration. Campus administration is usually open to student input and even work to ensure student representation at meetings and university events. If you feel like student representation is not a priority on your campus, take the time to sit down with key administrators and express how you feel and why student representation is important for the well-being of the university. The softest voice in the room can sometimes be the most effective. When meeting with administrators or politicians, understanding their perspective is critical in finding common ground and coming to a mutual and beneficial agreement.

As a diplomat, the way you deliver a message is critical. You must find a balance between being firm with your message while maintaining respectful dialogue. However, do not let diplomacy quiet you to a point where your opinion is overlooked or ignored in its entirety. At the same time, if you are too aggressive there's a good chance you will be written off and met with a lack of enthusiasm when it comes to working with administrators and other stakeholders. It's about being sharp with your message and convincing in your presentation. Here is an example of a student leader asking an administrator about school services:

"I feel as though the university provides services that help many people, in fact a friend of mine uses some of these services all the time. However, the university is cutting back on these services. You see it is essential for these services to be continued because classes are too big and no one is able to learn anymore. If no one is able to learn, what is education worth? Are you against learning!?"

Let's take a look at the paragraph above. If you were an administrator, are you certain that you understand what was just asked of you? The language seems to be that of someone who is well spoken, but the message is sloppy. The speaker has mentioned issues with services and education, but has not delivered a clear request. Furthermore, the speaker finished with what appears to be an attack. This message is like attempting to cut a steak with a butter knife. With enough work you might tear a piece, but it may be jagged, make a mess, and you might leave a bad impression. Instead, one should approach a request as follows:

"Higher education must be properly funded. A lack of funding is forcing campuses to shut down essential services that students need. Furthermore, without proper funding, classes become even harder for students to access. By effectively funding the university you can bring back essential services to the university and allow students to truly receive a world class education. Will you help find funding for the university?"

This second speaker has presented the points clearly. The university needs money to provide an education and essential services for students. The speaker further offers the opportunity to make a positive change rather than insulting or accusing and finishes the statement with a clear question. By following this method, the speaker has insured a clear communication of the problems and offered solutions.

A meaningful message delivered in a respectful manner, often hits home with the person you are speaking to. It is important to come off as respectful and knowledgeable, since students can sometimes be written off as naive or too young. That assumption could not be more wrong because students are often at the forefront of innovation and learning. In order to prove your point; speak in a way that is respectful, yet also honest and direct. It is crucial to make the distinction between a sharp or forward statement and a rude one. Diplomacy as a form of advocacy requires mutual respect. You will never be able to get what you want from a meeting if you enter the room looking to make a personal attack. Take the following example:

> *"Senator you are a failure as a representative, the only redeeming quality of your tenure is the fact that you accepted this meeting. Your legacy is pitiful and without doing what I am telling you, your days will be numbered and I could not be happier about that."*

Obviously this statement is incredibly rude and would likely cause you and your team to be asked to leave. This statement can easily be altered to be a sharp statement without being received so poorly as follows:

> *"Senator, we understand how busy you have been and really appreciate finally having a sit down with you. It is important that you help us with this initiative. We realize that you have not been supportive of this type of work in the past, but we truly believe that this initiative is different in that it addresses the problem. We would be eager to discuss any concerns you may have regarding the initiative so that we can work together."*

The above statement is presenting similar points, but is treating the representative with respect (that they may or may not deserve, but that you should give). The student leader still managed to call out the representative for not meeting with them and for not being a great representative. The difference is, they have done so in a respectful and professional manner; this is lobbying.

The Art of Lobbying

Lobbying is a skill that you can only develop by doing. The good news is that you have been lobbying your entire life. Every time you asked your parents for anything, tried to convince your teacher for extra credit, or your friend to share their lunch, you were lobbying.

Lobbying is a form of diplomacy where legislators are directly approached about an issue which plays a significant role in modern politics. As a student leader, lobbying is a skill that is just as important as delivering public speeches. Being an effective lobbyist will be invaluable as you meet with politicians, administrators, business leaders, or other individuals. On a campus level, lobbying can be used effectively to ensure your constituent's needs are heard by those that have the power to affect change.

The majority of university students have a relatively limited understanding of the programs and resources their university provides. These students lack the institutional knowledge that their peers who work for a campus program or hold a leadership position do. When an average student encounters a problem on campus, a few things can occur:

- They do nothing and do not fix the issue.
- They try and solve the issue on their own without seeking support.
- They reach out to a person or seek support from an office on campus.

The third choice is ideal, however, that is rarely the case and it's common for students to be met with inaction. For this reason, student leaders need to be strong and effective advocates. Regardless of how the student chooses to approach the issue, you as a student leader have the opportunity and, even more so, the obligation to take action. Understanding how to effectively lobby will ensure whatever action you take has a positive outcome.

Advocacy in Real Life

I began my career in student advocacy at the University of California, Riverside. In my first months as a student organizer, I was thrown into a state of turmoil. The stage had been set by huge tuition increases occurring for several years until 2011. Students were frustrated and feeling powerless. Student organizers at the time felt the pressure to act and so ensued the process of radical advocacy.

Protests and sit-ins occurred across the system. They were met with resistance as is typical with radical advocacy. Students at the University of California, Davis were pepper sprayed by campus police during a peaceful campus sit-in. Berkeley students were beaten by officers and Riverside students, upon their protest of the regents meeting, were met with riot gear and rubber bullets.

These violent responses are far too common when dealing with radical advocacy. While radical protests were taking place outside, indoor meetings were also taking place with any and all officials who would listen. Work was being done, but change was slow to come. Keep this in mind, as you work towards your goals; change will come, but it may not come as quickly as you would like. Despite the state of the university, students did not give up and continued organizing protests. The efforts of students continued on the ground as protesters from the Occupy Movement also took to the campuses to battle the privatization of the university system. In the 2012 elections, students came out in force. As mentioned earlier, this election was a game changer for student organizers because it forced everyone to take note of student power. An integral part of advocacy is flexing the power of your constituents. In both radical and diplomatic advocacy one person can be an advocate, but will be significantly more effective if they are backed with a powerful constituency.

The large student voter turnout in California showed everyone that students mattered. Oregon also claimed a top record of voter registration, working year round to ensure their public officials were aware of their student constituency. Once the movement had the backing of a huge voter turnout, the momentum began to shift.

The protests continued and meetings took place, both of which were taken more seriously because politicians and decision makers realized that students could play a huge role in the upcoming years and elections. Given this baseline of power, student protests were greeted with special committees and task forces rather than police brutality. Voter registration efforts definitely elevated the student's level of privilege when it came to the eyes of the decision makers. The advocacy continued and students saw years of tuition freezes.

When I was elected President of the University of California Student Association, we were able to engage in Board of Regent meetings, participate in state-wide committees, advocate for tuition freezes, and advocate for $15 million to be disbursed to underrepresented students. We were successful because we effectively used both radical and diplomatic advocacy.

Each aspect of advocacy, radicalism, diplomacy, and lobbying can be looked upon negatively if done incorrectly. Radicals are often earmarked as, well, radicals, and their concerns are sometimes not taken seriously. Use of the diplomatic approach in student organizing can be met with resistance. It is important that you keep your intentions pure and focused on your goals.

Once you gain an understanding of these two forms of advocacy you can begin to effectively work towards your goal. A mixture of these two forms of student organizing has been used throughout history.

When organizing as a student leader you must consider what you have at your disposal. It is people power not money that student organizers have, and when used properly this can be just as effective. Advocacy is not about notoriety, a story, or a way to enhance your own interests or aspirations. True advocacy is about representing your constituents by fighting for change that will make their lives better. Advocacy is not about you as a person; it is about the people you represent. At its core, advocacy is a selfless act for your community, constituency, and ultimately for a stronger and better future.

KEY CONCEPTS

1. Advocacy is about furthering the interests of a group of people or a cause and there are two ways to participate in student advocacy: radicalism and diplomacy.

2. Radicalism has its purpose within student government. It is often the only option for underrepresented communities and those who do not have the ability to access the system.

3. Diplomacy is about working with the system to effect change through meetings. This form of advocacy is excellent for being heard.

4. In order to affect change, your cause must be widely felt, deeply needed, and have real life implications.

5. Lobbying is a talent that you are always practicing that will allow you to send an effective message.

6. Do not get caught up in the glory of it all. Advocacy is for the betterment of your constituents, not the fulfillment of your own ego.

MY REFLECTION

KELSEY BREWER | STUDENT TRUSTEE
BOARD OF TRUSTEES, CALIFORNIA STATE UNIVERSITY

One of the most vivid memories I have of my childhood is walking to school with my grandmother when I was 8 years old. My grandmother was honestly the weirdest person I knew at the time, and that was part of the reason I loved her so much; she was just so different. That's what made her great. We stepped out of the house to a ground that was still wet from the rain the night before. My grandmother popped her shoes off (because who does not like walking barefoot in the rain?) and I was given permission to splash around in all of the puddles we encountered along the way. About halfway to my school, I noticed that my grandmother had fallen a couple yards behind me on the walk. I circled back and found her hunched over the place where my neighbors' lawns met the sidewalk. She was muttering quietly to herself as she picked earthworms up off the sidewalk and threw them back into the dirt. When she glanced up she noticed my perplexed face; she laughed and explained between giggles that the worms would die quickly if they did not make it back in the dirt.

I did not really get why worms were all of the sudden so much more important than my puddle splashing, but I just giggled back and dragged my grandmother along again. We continued on, stopping intermediately, to bend down and throw squirmy worms back into the soil. Having the attention span of, well, an eight-year-old, I became tired of this seemingly meaningless activity.

I questioned why were we wasting our time on worms, especially when we would not be able to get them all by the time the sun was fully shining. My grandmother did not respond and kept her silent rhythm of walking, bending, and throwing until we reached the schoolyard gates. As she gave me a hug and buttoned my jacket she very quietly and calmly said "We do it because it matters, Kelsey" She kissed my cheek and headed up the other side of the street, undoubtedly in search of more earthworms she could save.

It took years to understand the very simple lesson my grandmother was trying to teach me that day. It was not until an exasperated administrator asked me why I was causing such mayhem over a campus issue that only effected a few thousand of our 38,000 students. It was a good and fair question that I had not given a lot of thought to, yet here was this incredibly well-respected and powerful person asking me it none the less.

I thought on my feet and for some reason the first thing that came to my mind was, "…because it matters." Granted, that probably was not the most articulate or descriptive answer to her question…but it was the correct one. The reason we protest. The reason we march. The reason we sit in boring and seemingly endless meetings. The reason we stay up late practicing our talking points. The reason student leaders took the time to write this book. The answer to all of those "why do we do what we do" questions are the same. We do it because it matters. Because we matter. Because students matter. Being an advocate and a warrior for justice is so much more than a title or position.

It means that you occupy a privileged space where you have the opportunity to do something for other people who may not even know who you are. So do whatever you want to do with your time as a student leader. Just make sure that when it's all said and done... it mattered.

4. SHARED GOVERNANCE
KAREEM AREF | FORMER PRESIDENT
UNIVERSITY OF CALIFORNIA STUDENT ASSOCIATION

In the last chapter, we discussed the methods of advocacy, which can be used to achieve goals. Once you understand advocacy, you can begin to focus on how to best utilize this skill to your advantage as a student leader. Radicalism and diplomacy are amazing tools, but to achieve what? Your goals should be clear. During the election and appointment process, you will have made promises and committed to accomplish things that benefit the people you represent and serve. Although polarized political affiliations are common in student organizations, student leaders generally focus on the same central ideals:

- Accountability of administration to students.
- Increasing services for students.
- School pride and creating a positive campus culture.

The focus is to take these ideas and actually turn them into accomplishable goals by having a seat at the right meetings.

Getting Students Involved
When I was elected Vice President of External Affairs for the Associated Students of the University of California, Riverside, the office was on an upswing. We were lucky to have had several great leaders come into the office within a year or two. I knew the key to maintaining the

office's strength was to cultivate new leadership.

In student organizing, we typically have an abundance of two things. First, problems that need to be addressed. Second, students who care or would care if they knew about these issues. The key to successful campus leadership is using those together! I expanded my office from 4 members to over 100 by addressing these issues. While the office had grown immensely, it was structured so that each person had a specific duty or group which they fell into. If you are bringing in new people, it is vital you give them the appropriate information to get them going. There are many issues and there is always room for committees to address these issues. So develop opportunities for your constituents to get involved and allow them to have a voice on different matters.

In order to create positions, you need to think critically about your job and all the things you would like to accomplish. In the office of External Affairs, we focused on three main areas, legislative (primarily advocacy through diplomacy), Action (radical advocacy), and Engagement (voter registration). Within each of these categories there were specialties. Legislative affairs was divided into local and national. Action was split into community, labor, and multicultural. Voter registration was assigned multiple assistant directors to help coordinate different tasks. Each branch also had a committee. This structure allowed for many students to get engaged, and provided a very diverse student government.

Once the positions have been created, you need to start recruiting for each new position. The other essential part of structuring the office is to ensure opportunities for mentor-ship.

As a leader you should be working with everyone, but there will invariably be different levels of seniority. By building the office in this manner, you constantly allow for recruitment and for the training of not only your successor, but your second and third in command as well. This allows for easy transitioning and organizational continuity.

Getting the University Involved

After you have established a system to keep the students organized, you must then turn to your university's governmental structure. Across all educational systems, students usually outnumber university or school employees. Schools should be responsive to student concerns because the biggest stakeholders in the school are not the deans, chancellors, presidents, or regents, but the students. Some of you are lucky to have responsive administrators, others might not be; regardless of your situation you must take steps to ensure there is an institutional mean for students to demand responsiveness and have a say in the decision making process. It makes sense that a significant portion of the population should be represented at the decision making table. Students are that portion and they should have a seat right there with the administrators. This is the concept of Shared

Governance. It means that all stakeholders have a fair say in the decisions that impact their particular constituents. When we began speaking about advocacy, diplomatic advocacy was said to require some level of privilege. The goal of shared governance is to ensure that you and your constituents are not at the mercy of university officials. The road to attaining shared governance may vary and unfortunately, it is not as widespread as we would hope for. The United States Student Association adopted the pursuit of shared governance as one of their 2013-14 campaigns. While the road to achieve shared governance may differ, in its final form it should look relatively similar.

Whatever the governing body of your school, whether it the Board of Regents, Presidents, or Governors, you must establish a seat at the table for students. Effective shared governance is more than just being present; it's about having the power to implement actions in the university that benefit your students. I do not know if shared governance truly exists in any system of higher education, but I do know attempts are being made. Ideally you will be able to establish a system in which students have just as much say, or even a proportional say based on population, about what happens in the university.

Getting a Seat at the Table

If we take a look back in history, we can recall the colonies that would evolve into the United States, demanding "no taxation without representation." What did this mean? It meant that they wanted to have shared governance in establishing the laws and taxes. This can almost be equated to students demanding representation on tuition decisions. If we turn this historical event into a hypothetical one, what would have happened if the British had given the colonies representation in parliament?

The representative likely would have been outvoted. Shared governance is not a radical concept, at its core it is no more than acknowledging that students are not only fully capable and intelligent people, but can make educated decisions.

The United States Student Association recently worked on establishing more shared governance systems. California is filled with examples of shared governance. Take the University of California for instance. First and foremost, the Board of Regents (governing board of all the UC's) does have a sitting student regent. This student is a full member of the board who has voting power and access to all materials. They sit for two years, one as a nonvoting designate and one as a voting regent. While this position is a great step toward shared governance it alone is not enough because the student regent is never a deciding vote. In fact, most votes are unanimous with only the exception of the student regent.

Within the University of California, the statewide student association is given the authority to present at the regent's meetings, appoint students to system wide committees, and has several other powers that allow for oversight of the university. Together, these steps begin to establish a concept of shared governance.

At California State University, Fullerton the university was proposing a student fee increase. The student leaders at the time stood their ground and demanded a fair process. They involved themselves from the beginning creating a transparent and fluid process. By working with the administration and by utilizing the concept of Shared Governance the student leaders at CSUF turned this process into one of the most transparent student fee increases in the state. Could there be better models for Shared Governance? Probably. However, it is a great starting point.

Putting it all Together
At the end of the day, a student leader needs the ability to fight to affect change for their students. While advocacy plays a great role, if it is not passed on through generations, then nothing will be achieved for more than a few years. Training successors and getting students involved is essential. Once you have built this strong tradition, laying the groundwork for change may not be the most recognized aspect of the job, but it is about making change rather than recognition. There is no better

way to facilitate change than to have a system of shared governance in place.

KEY CONCEPTS

1. There are many issues and there is always room for committees to address these issues. So develop opportunities for your constituents to get involved and allow them to have a voice on different matters.

2. You have a lot of issues to deal with and a lot of students just waiting for the right cause, use these two together!

3. Shared Governance allows for those who are affected the most by decisions to have a say in the decision making process.

4. Not all shared governance is created equal. Fight for a meaningful cause and represent your constituent's in meetings.

5. Establishing a system of shared governance will essentially give you a hand in every student issue that will have to be solved at your institutions.

MY REFLECTION

KATY JOHNSON | STUDENT BODY VICE PRESIDENT
CALIFORNIA STATE UNIVERSITY, FULLERTON

As a student leader, shared governance is one of the most important aspects to keep in mind when preparing for your year in office. When the President and I talked about what the year would look like and what we wanted to work towards, communication, transparency and shared governance were among the most important to us. We knew that if we wanted to make big changes on campus, we would need to work with the other student leaders, organizations, staff and administration, in order to bring our ideas to fruition. It's not possible to accomplish all of your dreams and goals by yourself, nor should you think you can do everything alone. All great things that have happened in the world have happened through unity.

This year, within our Associated Students, we have implemented a mentality of shared governance and collaboration. Our organizations are working together to accomplish more than they have in the past. Students are more passionate and more involved in campus advocacy as well as working towards finding effective solutions. Our Board of Directors also wrote a resolution that urges educators to look into alternative learning outcomes for CSU students due to the rising cost of textbooks and required materials. This resolution went on to our Academic Senate committee which is made up of department chairs and university executives, and is being worked on by each stakeholder on campus. We are also working very closely with the university so that students are represented on all university wide committees.

For example, Cal State Fullerton is in the process of creating an Academic Master Plan. To do this, the students are working in committees alongside administration, faculty, and staff to put together a comprehensive plan for the university. We are fortunate that the university understands the importance of the student voice and are keeping students involved in these major decisions.

Throughout my experience, I have learned that communication is an important tool to exercise when trying to accomplish shared governance. Whether it is communication with students about advocacy, with administration about the student voice, or with fellow student leaders, communication can greatly aid in accomplishing shared governance. Creating good relationships with on campus partners is another important aspect that will help promote shared governance and make working together easier.

Student leadership has definitely been challenging, but at the same time, it has shaped me into who I am today. One of the greatest lessons I learned from student leadership can be related to a quote from the movie A League of Their Own.

"It's supposed to be hard, but hard is what makes it great."

5. CREATING YOUR TEAM
JUDITH MARTINEZ | FORMER STUDENT BODY PRESIDENT
SANTA CLARA UNIVERSITY

Have you ever heard the phrase, "you are the average of the five people you spend the most time with?" To some degree, this statement holds a valuable truth. A truth that is important to consider as a student leader when creating your team, and most importantly, when cultivating leadership within that team.

Whether your team is appointed or elected, chosen by you or an administrator, decided by the student body or a single nomination - there is one understanding across any school that underlines it all: you, as a team, have a purpose. You have a responsibility to represent a student body and advocate for the student voice. Who your team consists of may not be fully within your control; however, what your team is capable of, is. You have the ability to lead your team and ensure both their individual and collective success.

Selecting a Running Mate
Assume you are about to run in a campus wide election and you are ready to pick a running mate (which usually applies to the President and Vice President). The first thing to do is put together a list of questions to ask yourself and reflect on: Who do you pick? Should you go with someone who is popular, and can bring votes; or someone who has a clear passion? Someone with experience; or a recognized name? Someone who agrees

with your entire vision; or someone who will question parts of it? Someone you may not completely agree with, but you know can get the job done; or someone you see as a friend, but not with the best work ethic? These are all valid and reasonable questions to be asking yourself when selecting a running mate.

Before you decide to participate in elections, it is absolutely essential you develop a vision, goals, and a set of objectives you plan to carry out during your term if you are elected. If you do not have these in mind, then ask yourself, "why am I running?" If you do have a vision, goals, and a set of objectives, then a great question to follow is "who can be a partner in creating and fulfilling them?" For some, it may not be easy to find someone who you consider "popular" and "passionate" about student advocacy. For others, it may be a complete strategic mind game of trade-offs and what if's. No matter how you choose to go about selecting a running mate, keep in mind that a running partner is a true commitment. You want someone by your side that will support you until the end.

Prior to elections, my Vice President approached me to run with him. I felt honored and fortunately, we both had years of student leadership experience, including three years of student service at our own university. That was not the only reason I said "yes." I considered other factors that not only made the choice much easier, but ones that excited me to get to work. Take a look at the list below and ask yourself if you have considered the same when selecting your partner-to-be: These are the factors which I considered when I chose my running mate.

- Years of student leadership experience on campus
- Affiliation with student groups I was not affiliated with
- Had a similar vision as I did, yet still developed his own vision
- Shared passion for leaving our university better than when we started
- Well spoken, well dressed, well respected
- Great work ethic and had strengths that I considered my weaknesses
- Fun to be around and outgoing

These are just a few reasons why I agreed to run with my vice president. More than that, I knew he had similar reasons as to why he chose me. Finding a running mate for an election can be overwhelming. You can seek advice from others on who to choose as your running mate but understand that you are the only person who can choose who will be the best fit. Talk to the people or person you are considering and actually have a conversation. Are they interested? Do they want to join you? What does a partnership look like? What are your goals? What are theirs? At the end of the day, you have to consider everything. The ticket and the platform. The person and the title. The long nights and the early mornings. The defeats and the victories. Who do you want by your side through all of it?

Creating Your Board/Cabinet

Selecting a running mate is just one of the many decisions student leaders will have to make. Selecting an entire board and team to work with is another. If you find yourself in the position to choose your board, you have complete freedom to create a team you envision as "ideal." If you are not in a position to choose your board, do not fret. Spearhead the selection process with a positive mentality, an innovative outlook, and a clear sense of your mission and philosophy as a leader.

If you are hand selecting your team, be prepared to be confronted with some difficult choices. You may find yourself struggling with biases, favoritism, opinions from others, fear of making the "wrong choice", and even self-doubt in your own ability as a leader. These are all normal feelings, and a good sign that what you are doing is important to you. But all feelings aside, you have a responsibility to fulfill and that includes building a team. So how do you go about it? Whether you already have a few people in mind, or have no clue where to start, there are a few practical systems your organization may have in place already, or systems you can put in place yourself to help you and future student leaders:

- Elections/student body nominations
- School wide applications
- Interviews
- Active recruiting

- Recommendations from other student leaders, mentors, faculty, staff, and administration

All the above can be great ways to make it easier for you to decide. It is important to narrow down your search to a select few who embody what you envision. When it came time to create my team, there were a handful of things I kept in mind. Values are just as important as a person's vision or list of accomplishments. When I chose my team, I based my selection process on four important values I was committed to having as integral foundations of the team: diversity, passion, empathy, and integrity.

Diversity
Diversity is broader than simply ethnicity, race or gender. What I particularly mean, and looked for, was diversity in opinion. Diversity brings innovation; and for me, there was nothing more exciting than the thought of a multitude of thoughts, opinions, and interpretations coming together and discussing innovative, creative ways to address student needs on our campus. Consider having the various voices, perspectives, and concerns of your peers represented at your own table. School aside, when you think about any successful business, you should not be surprised as to why diversity is such a common topic among employers or companies looking to hire. When you gather people from all stages and ages of life, from a spectrum of experiences, races, and sexes, you also create the potential to build a great team filled with diverse thinkers.

Passion

Passion can manifest itself in a variety of ways. For me, it meant action. I knew someone was passionate by their actions. Coming into my position as President, there were so many things ahead that neither I nor anyone on the team could foresee. There were many ups and downs. I freaked out at the thought of being unable to control everything and every outcome. What gave me peace of mind, both as a student and student leader, was the thought and the belief that we as a team could get through it because we were passionate about what we were doing.

Staying up late to finish a proposal, sitting down for the twentieth time to approve a budget, or desperately looking for blue tape, paint, and poster paper - it was all worth it because they were all actions that got us toward what we passionately believed in.

During my time as a student leader, I've come across leaders who were extremely passionate and those who were in it for their resume. While a resume builder will flake, falter, and ultimately fail at the sign of an obstacle, a passionate person can overcome any obstacle a head of them and continue moving forward.

Empathy

When working and interacting with people in general, practicing empathy will get you far, because it means you can put yourself in someone else's shoes. In student leadership, and everything else in life for that matter, this is extremely important. Whether it's the concerns of your constituents, the worries of your team, the opinions of the administration, or maybe even the anxieties of a potential group you want to collaborate with. Thinking about where someone else is coming from will put you in a position to take actions that are inclusive and meaningful for both you and that person.

Empathy allows you to support someone who is having a rough time or step in when someone needs it. In return, you'll have created a dynamic where you should feel comfortable and confident enough to ask for support if and when you find yourself having a hard time. Empathy, however, is not sympathy. Sympathy is an emotional response to a person's situation. Empathy is being able to understand that person's perspective and how it is altered by situational changes. A strong team recognizes this difference.

Integrity

Of all the four values, integrity is the one I regard as most important when it comes to authentic leadership and is equally essential to truly being a public servant. In building a team, I wanted to bring together a group that was true to their word and held me accountable. Whether it is trusting everyone would show up on time for meetings; trusting everyone would make grades to stay on board; trusting people will do what they say they will do;

and trusting each other's skills and talents to get the job done. Without trust, there would not have been any progress.

The biggest challenge for me was trusting another person's opinion and listening, even if it did not align with my own. I was not interested in having "Yes" leaders on board, so surrounding myself with people who could disagree without being disrespectful made a huge difference in how we as a team collaborated. Regardless of our disagreements, we still managed to accomplish all of our tasks in a timely and respectful manner, mainly due to the trust and confidence we had developed.

Delegation: Building a Team

Bringing a group of people to work together is one thing; building each person up as a leader is another. Play off people's strengths and learn to encourage others to rise above what they consider their weaknesses. Whether you are creating your team or fostering teamwork, find out what each person is great at and what things they can accomplish. As important as it is to have someone focus on what they do best, one of the rewarding privileges of student leadership is growing as a team toward a common goal. Part of that growth can mean challenging yourself to go beyond what you may have thought was ever possible. Whether that's encouraging someone shy to lead a meeting, or supporting someone who may not think they are the best public speaker to make an announcement, build your team, and you build yourself.

Cohesion: Creating a Culture

If your school is anything like mine, your entire organization consists of students who either ran for a position and were elected, nominated, appointed, or were recommended by an administrator or staff member. My university had a very diverse culture which brought in a wide range of experiences, which can be intimidating for some students. Different, can sometimes be mistaken by some student leaders as difficult. It might be difficult to get along; difficult to work as a team; difficult to get anything done. So what do you do if you find yourself or your team in a place that sees diversity as more of a burden than a blessing? How do you foster a successful team dynamic in whatever group you find yourself? Consider some of the things below and ask yourself if they could make a difference for you and your organization if they have not already:

Retreats

The student organization at my university has a tradition of having one large retreat at the beginning of each academic school year, and two smaller quarter retreats at the beginning of each new academic quarter. These retreats excited everyone for the year/quarter ahead, and ensured everyone was on the same page in terms of the mission and goals of the organization. It also provided a quick escape to reflect and be grateful for the opportunities that we had.

Sharing & Leading

During my time in office, I would occasionally share with my board articles, news clips, or short videos that inspired me or were relevant to what we were facing as a team. In turn, I loved hearing quotes, comics, or even random memes that brightened my day. Sharing gives the feeling of inclusivity, and sometimes, the heart of disagreements on boards or teams can be because someone does not feel "part" of the team. Having consistent scheduled meetings or outings together as a team and one on one check-ins will also strengthen your bond as a team.

Life beyond the position

Remember that everyone on your team, including you, has a personal life. Small things like celebrating birthdays, significant moments, accomplishments, or even grabbing team dinners is a great way to build team morale and build a sense of support and rapport with one another. Taking time to give recognition to people in your organization/team creates a sense of accomplishment, acknowledgment, and appreciation for others and their work. During my term, our organization had an "all-star jar" that served as a trophy to whomever we felt did a remarkable job with something, whether it was after a rough week, sealing a deal, or keeping cool in a tough situation, it was great to bring to light and recognize someone for their hard work.

This was also a great way to inspire others to make efforts to go above and beyond. Sharing class schedules and important dates with the team also made a difference. Receiving a "good luck!" text from a board member during one of my hardest finals gave me such a sense of relief though it took only a second from their day. At the end of the day, you are all students as well as leaders.

Create a Safe Zone

Creating a space where you and the others around you can feel safe to be vulnerable makes a world of a difference. There were many moments during my time in office where I felt being vulnerable and authentic set the tone and set an example for others to follow. The same can be said for the examples set by others that inspired me to follow suit. When you put yourself in a position to be vulnerable, you create a space for others to do the same and open up about things that can contribute to the success of your team. Vulnerability can foster a sense of trust that is essential for any team to succeed. During one of my retreats, the leader of our group shared a really touching and personal story about his life. Immediately you could see tensions easing up and people bonding through sharing their own stories. Sometimes all it takes is that first step in showing vulnerability to create a safe zone. Creating a team is not necessarily about picking the right people, it's about empowering the people around you no matter what group you are in. My Vice President always had a great way of reminding us it's not group work, it is teamwork. A group consists of individuals working toward and fulfilling individual goals or tasks; a team is a group of people who share a common purpose, challenges, goals, and share a responsibility for the team's success. It takes time and effort to put together a dream team, but remembering your overall mission, values, and responsibilities makes it a little easier. By keeping a goal-oriented focus and holding people accountable, you can create a team that not only works together, but achieves remarkable things together.

KEY CONCEPTS

1. Who your team consists of may not be fully within your control; however, what your team is capable of is under your control. You may not have the ability to handpick your entire team, but you do have the responsibility of leading your team and striving for results.

2. The people you work and surround yourself with will play a large role on the results you produce.

3. When choosing a running mate, keep in mind your vision, mission, and goals, as well as theirs. Do they align? Partnership is a true commitment.

4. Diversity, passion, empathy, and integrity are great starting points when looking for people with whom to surround yourself.

5. Build your team, and you build yourself.

6. Creating a team is not about picking the right people, it's about empowering the people around you no matter what group.

MY REFLECTION

JONNY LEGGETT|FORMER STUDENT BODY VICE PRESIDENT
CALIFORNIA STATE UNIVERSITY, FULLERTON

In the spring of 2013 my partner Rohullah Latif and I had won our election to become the California State University Fullerton, Associated Student Inc. President and Executive Vice President. After a short celebration we geared up ready to work. Our first task was to assemble a team, an unstoppable team, a team of the best student leaders we could find around campus. We wanted to be different, we wanted to make a change, and we wanted to build something that no other administration had ever done before.

When you get in this type of role you have the urge to pick some of your closest friends for these positions. These people have helped campaign for you and they were the first people to firmly believe in you as a leader. You know you can trust them, but sometimes you have to do the hard thing. If you want to build the greatest team you can assemble you need to stay true to yourself and your mission.

As applications came in I knew one of my fraternity brothers was going to apply to one of our executive team positions. He was a brilliant man and exercised exemplary leadership in all aspects. As my partner and I were going through interviews something did not feel right. Another candidate had come into the hardest interview we could create (we deliberately placed all of the candidates in a

55

chair placed in the center of the room, while 5 people interviewed them) and blew us away. This candidate was a former presidential nominee.

As I sat face to face in the interview with the man who had ran for the same position, the man who kept us up at night and on our toes, something hit me. The past did not matter. We both wanted the exact same thing. We wanted to make a difference on our campus. I knew he would get the job done and would out-work anyone else. One of the most difficult conversations I had was with my fraternity brother, letting him know he did not get the position, and instead, I was giving it to the man I had campaigned against for the last month.

When creating your team, it is important to not just look at the past, but more importantly to envision the future. You as the leader can navigate the waters around previous uncomfortable situations because together you are working for something bigger than yourself. You have to trust yourself and trust that you are the amazing leader that you know you are.

Teamwork is the ability to work together toward a common vision. The ability to direct individual accomplishment toward organizational objectives. It is the fuel that allows common people to attain uncommon results. ~Andrew Carnegie

6. REPRESENTING MORE THAN YOURSELF

DANIEL CLARK | FORMER PRESIDENT
CALIFORNIA STATE STUDENT ASSOCIATION

As a student leader you are an elected official. You are a representative of your constituents, and they are often judged based on you and your actions. How you dress, behave, and communicate are all important facets of this job. You are "the student" so whenever there's a committee that needs someone, you're the one they will call. Whenever there is a problem that needs a solution, you're the one they will call. Whenever the media needs a sound-bite from a student, again, you're the one they're going to call. In these scenarios, it's always important to be the most professional.

First Impressions Matter
Nine times out of ten, an individual is going to judge you on your appearance within seconds of meeting you. People will judge you based on what you are wearing/not wearing, body language, and nonverbal communication. You have one opportunity at a first impression and the last thing you want is for a bad first impression to ruin your reputation.

There is a concept known as the halo effect that comes into play when individuals meet you for the first time. Any other subsequent encounters that they have with you will be dictated by this effect.

The halo effect means if someone's first encounter with you is positive, they will still think highly of you even if there are mishaps along the way. This is also important when they see the first visual impression of you. The halo effect is important when it comes to brand marketing and the product you are selling. The product you're selling is not something you buy on the shelf or at the store, the product is you.

Any behaviors that take away from the product you're selling will have detrimental effects that could take months or years to repair. While the halo effect is very important there is another effect in play known as the horn effect.

The horn effect is the exact opposite of the halo effect; if an individual finds something they do not like about you, regardless of what it is, they will have a negative mindset when it comes to working with or interacting with you. While you cannot control everything, your mannerisms and professionalism is something you can control.

"Dress for the job you want, not the job you have."

This age old saying is important. An individual is going to look at you first before they speak and will immediately judge you based on that. Professional attire is one form of nonverbal communication and something that you will be judged on. When you meet with campus administrators, business administrators, or elected officials, it is important to take the time and dress appropriately.

Looking professional not only boosts your confidence but also instills confidence in them about your abilities and attitude.

Professional and Business Casual Attire

Professional Attire

A lot of factors go into what defines professionalism. Professionalism in Humboldt, California and the dress attire associated with that culture may be a lot different from the dress attire in Miami, New York, or Los Angeles. Professional attire is geographic in nature. Since professionalism differs between different cultures, people, and locations, you have to approach it from a very wide lens. There is a wide array of different styles of clothing and unless you are very familiar with the individual or association you are encountering, it is always best to use caution and dress conservatively. Sometimes you will also hear the term "Business casual." This refers to a less formal traditional business wear but still displays a business like impression. Let's start with professional and end with business casual attire.

Professional Attire for Men

Grooming

Ensure all body hair is neat, tidy, and combed. Comb your hair and try to ensure that it does not touch your collar. Don't be afraid to rock a man bun if you have long hair, but understand that certain folks you are dealing with may look down on it. When it comes to facial hair make sure it is neat and not unruly. Cleaning up is a must for men with beards. Try not to go any longer than a size 2 on the clippers and remove any loose hairs around the neck as well. Trim the nose hairs, ear hairs, and the eyebrows. Earrings aren't the most unprofessional accessory you could wear, but it certainly isn't the most professional thing you should wear either. I highly recommend earrings stay off during professional encounters. Your fingernails need to remain trimmed and clean at all times.

Suit Style

In a professional setting a suit should be neutral color and should have a solid or subtle pattern. Colors that are acceptable are dark gray, light gray, navy, and brown. Black is typically viewed as more formal, but is also acceptable. Ensure that your jacket remains buttoned while you're standing and unbuttoned while you're seated. Only the top button remains buttoned except when you are sitting. Ensure that the pants you are wearing match the color of your suit top. Adding different colors may look slightly tacky if you are not careful. The bottom of your pants should touch the front of your shoes and fall back to the middle of the heel when you're standing. If it doesn't, your suit is either too short or long.

Suits don't need to be particularly expensive. If money is tight, then a black suit is recommended as it can virtually match with anything. Don't be afraid to shop the clearance racks and tailor a suit to meet your needs. A tailor can be your best friend; find one and develop a relationship with them.

Colored Shirts, Ties, and Bow Ties

Your shirt should complement your suit and not stand out excessively. A white shirt or a muted color shirt works well with any suit color. Muted colors include light blue, light pink, light purple, and light green. Long sleeve shirts are essential and ensure the shirt has no wrinkles in the collar or the cuffs. The collar should be loose enough so that one finger can fit in the neck line.

Your tie and its width are also important when selecting your outfit. Once the tie is tied, it should land on top of your belt or be very close to it. Bow-ties offer an opportunity to subtly stand out compared to your colleagues. Once I learned how to tie a bow tie, I was a big fan and everyone immediately noticed my bow ties during events.

YouTube has great instructional videos on how to tie bow-ties if you have never tied one before. The colors you chose to wear can also have different meanings. There has been extensive research on the psychological effect colors can have. Red is seen as a power color, blue has a calming effect, and black is seen as more formal.

Shoes/ Socks

You can tell a lot about a person by the way they take care of their shoes. Shoes complete your outfit. Select dark shoes that complement your suit that do not distract from it. It is important to ensure that your shoes are polished and clean at all times. Shoes can make or break an outfit, so learn how to polish your shoes correctly or find someone who can shine your shoes. Matching the colors of your shoes to your belt matters, brown shoes, brown belt and black shoes, and black belt. It is important that your socks match the color of your suit. If you're wearing a black suit, then wear black socks. A blue suit goes with blue socks and a brown suit goes with brown socks. Never wear white socks with a suit or dress pants. Socks should be long enough to reach your calf so that when you cross your legs, no skin shows. Try to add a little flavor with your socks if you can. For example, I had a meeting with a businesswoman and I wore a charcoal suit, teal dress shirt, with teal & white striped tie, brown belt, brown shoes, and some funky bright polka dotted green/blue/teal dress socks. I then purposely sat and crossed my legs. The first words that came out of her mouth were "oh my, I love your style and socks!"

Accessories

The only accessories appropriate with a suit are professional style watches (no sports watches), cufflinks to go with your shirt if needed, and a pocket handkerchief, which definitely adds more style to your wardrobe.

Business Casual for Men

Tops

A sports coat with a collared shirt and no tie would be appropriate attire for Business Casual. It would also be appropriate to wear professional short sleeve polos, tucked into your pants. For business casual style events ties and bow-ties are not necessary, but feel free to mix and match your own style. Tucking in your shirt completes the look and it will make your belt stand out.

Bottoms

Khakis or solid color slacks would work well for pants. Ensure that they are creased down the middle and have no visible wrinkles.

Belt and shoes

Your belt and shoes should match your attire and since you are not wearing a tie, your belt should stand out more. Leave the athletic, casual shoes at home, and wear your more formal shoes. This next portion on professional and casual attire for women is written by my co-author Judith Martinez.

Professional Attire for Women

Grooming

Ladies, your hairstyle should be fairly simple and kept away from your face. Neutral makeup is appropriate. Fingernails can be short and medium length, but be careful about long fingernails. They can look inappropriate and impractical while working and if your nail polish is chipped be sure to fix it.

Clothing

A two-piece business suit is always appropriate for any professional occasion. The color should be something simple such as black, gray, dark gray, or navy. The sleeve should be at or just below your wrist. Avoid skirts that are too tight and have high slits. If you decide to wear pants instead of a business skirt; Capri & cropped pants should be avoided to ensure that your pants match your top.

Blouse

A blouse or a camisole is an appropriate shirt to wear under your suit. It is also wise to wear a conservative neckline with the shirt. Your blouse should be long enough to be tucked in-to your suit pants. Colors such as white and muted color shirts are also appropriate. Muted colors include light blue, pink, off white or cream, green, and purple.

Shoes/ Hosiery

Avoid any sandals, strapped shoes, stilettos, and platform shoes and wear closed-toe low heel pumps. Hosiery should match your skin tone or be a neutral color.

Accessories

While dangling or hoop style earrings look great they are not what we would call professional. Any excessive piercings in the earlobe or anywhere else in the ear should be taken out. Watches should be business appropriate and if possible avoid the more-flashy accessories.

Business Casual for Women

Tops
A blazer or a suit jacket works well for business casual. As for shirts, a blouse or camisole will still work along with sweaters such as cardigans and knit sweaters. When it comes to colors stick with the lighter more muted colors even in business casual settings.

Bottom
Dress pants or khakis are acceptable for business casual environments. While Capri pants are comfortable they should be avoided when selecting your outfit. The same rules for professional dress also apply to skirts again. They should not be too revealing, not too tight, and avoid any high slits.

Belt and shoes
Your belt and shoes should match the style of dress you are wearing. Wear a leather belt and leather shoes. Athletic shoes are inappropriate.

Nonverbal Communication
Nonverbal communication, the behavior behind it, and the science of it all started with Charles Darwin "The Expression of the Emotions in Man and Animals." Since

then, the science behind it has exploded and numerous non-verbal communication studies have been tested on the effects it has on individuals. Nonverbal communication is the combination of thousands of nonverbal cues. There are many different types of nonverbal communication methods which include the following:

Eye contact

Eye contact is the most important form of nonverbal communication. Eye contact has three main purposes when communication is taking place. It gives feedback and provides an opportunity for you to give feedback. When you do not maintain eye contact it could result in disinterest, disrespect, and the message may not be received properly. Direct eye contact in certain cultures defines trust. However, in other cultures direct eye contact is disrespectful. Understanding your environment plays a critical role in representing yourself. Finally, eye contact provides cues for when a person is done speaking. As a student leader, maintaining eye contact with officials, is a display of confidence. It is also important to maintain eye contact with the audience when giving speeches.

Body Movements (Kinesics)

Similar to eye contact, body movements can relay information about a person's emotion or attitude. Imagine you see person A and person B walking down the sidewalk. Person A is walking fast with his head up, smiling and acknowledging people, while person B is walking slowly with his head down and avoiding eye contact with everyone. From afar you could maybe get the sense that person A is on a mission and out to take on the world as oppose to person B. Think of body movements as clues in the giant puzzle of interpersonal communication. The study of body movement and kinesthetic is divided into three different categories which are: adaptors, affect displays and emblems.

Adaptors

Think of adaptors as a way to get feedback about how a person is feeling. When a person scratches their head, adjusts their glasses constantly, fidgets in their seat, or constantly bites their fingernails, they represent the individual's feelings. These behaviors are subconscious and we act without even realizing it. Seeing these in meetings can help you understand what a person is really trying to say. Do one of your student leaders look nervous? Are campus administrators fidgeting in their seats when you speak? This can be useful information when you are conducting business.

Affect Displays

Affect displays are facial expressions or gestures that can give you a glimpse into their mood. The beauty of affect displays is that they are universal and can be understood regardless of language. You can get a sense of a person's expression when they look happy, sad, frightened, disgusted, surprised, or angry, all by just looking at the cues they give you. Be aware of the affect displays you are showing to the world, especially during interviews, speeches, or meetings.

Emblems

Emblems are gestures that are used to communicate with an individual. Some emblems are recognized worldwide, however, cultural context can have different meanings. Understand your constituent's culture and you will understand what emblems are appropriate, especially if you are presenting or introducing yourself to a cultural organization on campus.

Posture

Posture can indicate how a person feels, their opinion on the subject of what you're saying, or their own reactions to what is being communicated. Posture can be broken down into two different forms: open and closed. Open posture can communicate exactly what it implies, open communication and an open interest of the topic. Open communication implies that you are not closed off to the person speaking. Closed posture on the other hand has a lot of different meanings and is the exact opposite of open posture communication. Pay close attention to a person's posture when they are speaking to you. Sitting up straight and leaning in to show interest are great examples of good posture. However, slouching in a chair, arms folded, walking with a slouch could all be viewed as negative. These are especially crucial during meetings where everyone's eyes are on you.

Paralinguistic

Paralinguistic is best understood as "it's not just what you say, it's how you say it." Whether we realize it or not when we speak, people are picking up on subtle hints. Things such as the tone of your voice, emphasis on certain words, timing, pace, volume, casting or radiating certain emotions or cues. These can indicate whether you're frustrated, angry, confident, or sarcastic. These signals are very important when you're speaking. During speeches emphasizing particular words can really drive your message when you are communicating with campus administrators or the student body.

KEY CONCEPTS

1. As a student leader you are an elected official, you are a representation of your constituents, always represent yourself in a way that meets the obligations you have to your constituents.

2. Individuals will judge you immediately upon meeting you; make sure they are left with a great first impression.

3. First impressions are great, but developing a relationship is just as important.

4. Professional attire is important if you want people to take you seriously. Keep in mind, this varies by geographic region and campus culture.

5. Nonverbal communication is a dynamic process that includes eye contact, body movement posture, and personal space.

MY REFLECTION

FILIPE CARVALHO | MEMBER OF THE BOARD OF DIRECTORS
UNITED STATES STUDENT ASSOCIATION

It's 6 AM, a cold Massachusetts day in early march. I am skipping school today, but not for reasons that allow me to sleep in. After fighting the urge to doze off in the shower, I gel up my unruly hair, and brush my teeth. Now, I'm debating which suit I should wear. Gray with silver pinstripes? Tricky, but I like it. Now I just have to make sure I wear a shirt that matches- light blue works and it pairs well with that navy tie I just bought. Where did I put that watch? Oh yeah, in the dark corners of my desk drawer. It does not even tell time anymore, must need new batteries, oh well, it's not like anyone uses a watch to tell time anymore. Time for the finishing touches. Suit jackets are nothing in the face of a New England cold front, have to throw on the overcoat for this occasion, I cannot look silly with a winter coat now. Finally, I need something my messenger bag to carry my stuff. Never grab a backpack because they ruin the fabric of suits, they ruin the look too. I am definitely going to have a new LinkedIn picture by the end of today.

There are few times in the year that I do wear a full suit; job interviews and lobby visits. Regardless of your role as a student organizer, president, senator, activist, when you walk into an elected leader's office your age is inherently working against you. As students we have to be armed with more than just sharp arguments, relevant facts, and compelling stories to earn the respect of our elected officials and the greater public as well. After all, not only does our age group vote in incredibly low rates, but we are sometimes stereotyped as entitled, lazy, and incapable of grasping the complexity of political matters.

Unfortunately, this will put you on thinner ice than most when dealing with people in power. Along with your materials and ideas, appearances matter. As student leaders, you are counted upon to represent your fellow students. It is therefore best for you to represent the student body by dressing for success and acting in a professional manner. It is important to put your best foot forward when in important meetings and situations. Dress like someone who has power, because you do. And of course, there is a confidence boost that comes with putting on a tailored suit over a crisp, freshly pressed shirt.

In the above narrative, I was preparing for a visit to the State house for our annual higher education advocacy day. I was also tasked with giving a speech. There is something about a clean suit that eases the nerves and instills a certain level of bravado. It is easy to see why so many powerful people are constantly in their power suits. I do not condone the power trip, but next time you need to do powerful things with powerful people, reach for the suit.

7. ETHICS, DILEMMAS, & TOUGH DECISIONS

JUDITH MARTINEZ|FORMER STUDENT BODY PRESIDENT
SANTA CLARA UNIVERSITY

Whether you are a freshman and just joining the ranks, or a senior with years of experience, it is a privilege to have the amount of influence and power you have as a student leader. What really matters is what you do with it. When you think of your position, what responsibilities immediately come to mind? A budget? University improvements? Choosing a board? Fees and student spending? These may all be the tough decisions that come to mind, but choosing how you get there can be the toughest of them all.

Terms like right, wrong, fair, and just are common in the world of student leadership. It's important to understand what these terms can mean and how they can differ depending on any given situation you encounter as a student leader. The following examples are taken from Kori Lennon, a student leader from Santa Clara University, and my Vice President of Public Relations at Santa Clara University during my time in office. She dedicated her entire senior year creating case studies surrounding ethics in student government. The following examples and posed questions are her own and the Santa Clara University Markkula Center for Applied Ethics.

Scenario 1: Appointing A Cabinet

Marcus is the president of his student government. He and his running mate, Janelle, just won a tense and hard-fought election for the president and vice president positions.

Many excellent candidates ran, and the election was exceedingly close. Marcus is now faced with the task of appointing an executive cabinet. The executive cabinet is made up of the elected President, Vice President, Senate Chair, and 3 appointed members. Marcus was a member of the executive cabinet for the last two years, and understands that the dynamics of the executive cabinet sets the tone for the entire organization. He wants to get it right. All four of the opposing candidates in the presidential election had said they would be willing to take other positions if they did not win the race. They are all highly qualified individuals with significant student government experience. Their knowledge could be very valuable on the executive cabinet, and they could contribute to the backing of their campaign supporters. Marcus also feels it is important to include his opponents for the sake of organizational unity, since fostering unity is one of the main goals of student government. Despite their high potential, Marcus is seriously concerned that there might be resentment after his victory in the contentious election. In past years, he witnessed great candidates lose the election, take a position on the executive cabinet, and then spitefully contribute very little to the organization.

Marcus also has the option of hiring individuals who chose only to apply for positions. He knows that some of his most ardent campaign supporters applied for positions and would passionately share and support his vision in their work. They have much less experience than the presidential candidates, but Marcus does not doubt their energy and enthusiasm. They worked very, very hard for him, and he feels indebted. Marcus thinks that he will hire one opposing candidate and one supporter, to balance each other out, but cannot decide how to fill the crucial third spot.

What would you do in Marcus's position? Should he extend an olive branch, go for experience, and risk a resentful ex-candidate holding the team back? How should he negotiate rewarding his supporters? What factors do you think take priority when assembling a team after an election?

In this example with Marcus, how are some ways we can define what is "right" and what is "fair"? When my VP and I won our election, we wanted to take everyone and everything into consideration when it came time to create our team. This includes similar scenarios Marcus faced in the example above. We were still confronted with finding the "best fit" for our applicants. What served as a guiding light for us was considering what we envisioned, our end goal, and making sure we knew what we wanted and agreeing about it. We wanted a strong team; but strength does not always mean experience. We wanted a fresh perspective; but fresh did not have to mean zero history with the organization. We considered things from team dynamics, to what each person would bring to the table, strengths, weaknesses, contacts, majors, and their standing as a student. If you find yourself confronted with a similar situation as Marcus, keep these things in mind and consider the year ahead of you in office.

Scenario 2: Campaign Ethics

Olivia is the Community Relations Executive Coordinator for her university's student government. She recently made the decision to run for next year's Student Body President, and has a couple months to prepare for the election process. Because Olivia is already an executive member of the student government, she knows the election timeline at the beginning of the year, far before it is publicly advertised.

Olivia is passionate about student government, and wants to make a difference at her university. Most students do not yet know or care when the election is happening, but Olivia has already begun to prepare. From the start of the year, she spends hours at her desk in the office, brainstorming ideas for her campaign platform.

Olivia realizes that many of her ideas fit into the duties in her current role as Community Relations Executive Coordinator, and decides to begin to implement them now. She knows the initiatives would be great examples to use during the campaign season. Olivia has also mapped out the entire year of events for the Community

Relations Branch, and saves the best, most popular events for the few weeks before the elections. Despite the fact that the events could take place in the fall, Olivia decided to delay them until the spring, to better boost her public appeal and presence in the days before the election.

As she delves further into the planning process, Olivia begins to feel a little uneasy. No one else is planning for elections yet, because no one else knows the timeline. She wonders if it is fair that she already started the process. She was not intentionally trying to get a leg up on the competition, but starts to question if she's doing the right thing. Olivia fervently believes that the new initiatives she is planning to implement in Community Relations will positively impact the student body, but she wonders if it is wrong to have the explicit goal of supporting her campaign. What would you do in Olivia's position? Would you continue to plan the campaign, or set it aside until later? Is it fair that Olivia uses her inside information to begin planning earlier?

Should she plan initiatives with the intention of supporting her future campaign? Is it wrong to delay events to line up with elections? How do you negotiate the balance of campaigning while still in office?

Many student leaders can relate to Olivia. As a student leader already in office with the intention of running for another office, or another seat in the future, questions and feelings of uneasiness like what Olivia encountered are more common than not. If you find yourself in a similar position to Olivia, consider asking yourself, "what kind of situation are you dealing with?" and "how does that affect other things?" For example, if Olivia were to focus her time and energy on the initiatives she does not intend to actually put into effect until the future, how does that impact the team she is working with currently? Can Olivia actually say she is present and aware to what is happening with her board if she is busy strategizing for the future? Whatever your thoughts are about Olivia, there is a balance of holding your current position and the hope of holding another. One approach can be taking on projects and priorities one at a time. If you are in office to fulfill a particular set of responsibilities and tasks, it's a good idea to fulfill those responsibilities and tasks to the best of your ability. Strategizing for a possible future rather than staying present to what is in front of you may make your duties, and obligations to your constituents, a more difficult task than it needs to be.

Scenario 3: Caught in the Middle

Karina is the Senate Chair on her university's Associated Students board. As Senate Chair, she serves on both the Senate and The Associated Students Executive Cabinet. Karina supervises the Senate Committee Chairs and the general operations of the legislative branch. In her position on the executive cabinet, Karina works with the members of the Judicial and Executive Branch: The Chief Justice, President, Vice President, and Commissioners, to guide and develop the mission of the organization as a whole. Recently, proposed changes to student government bylaws have put the Executive Cabinet and the Senate at odds. The Senate disapproves of the strict attendance policy encouraged by the Executive Cabinet. The committee chair argues the policy is too paternalistic and shows little faith in the leadership of senators. They also point out that the Executive Cabinet has made a habit of strongly encouraging the Senate to pass resolutions, and they are beginning to push back. The Executive Cabinet believes a stricter attendance policy will inspire the small but inevitable cohort of slacker Senators to fulfill their duties, strengthening the organization as a whole. At the last Senate meeting, the debate degenerated into a yelling match. Karina thinks that both sides raise excellent, but opposite, points and that neither seems able to understand the opposing point of view.

Karina represents both branches, and now feels trapped in the middle. What would you do in Karina's position? How would you balance representing the Committee Chairs and Senate with the Executive Branch? Should one role take priority? Is the Executive Cabinet overstepping its bounds?

Even if you have never been in Karina's position, you can empathize with what she is confronted with in some shape or form. Being "stuck in the middle" or between a "rock and a hard place" is not unique to student leadership. If you do see yourself in Karina's shoes in your organization, I invite you to remember one thing: you are a capable, intelligent human being and you are in this student leadership position because others believe the same. So with that, have confidence in yourself, your voice, and your opinion. Also keep in mind what you are committed to. As important as it is to follow the mission, and vision of your organization, it is equally important to follow your own beliefs in order to uphold your position. What you value as this year's officer may not be the same values your predecessors had or your successors will have in mind. Apart from this, do not be afraid to initiate a conversation with everyone involved. Is it a good idea to hold a meeting where everyone is present? Would giving everyone an opportunity to share their thoughts help clear up any miscommunication? Is this really about X, or is it actually about Y? Do not feel intimidated if you find yourself in the middle and always remember you have mentors and advisors with whom you can turn.

Scenario 4: Unfair Funding?

Claire is the Finance Commissioner on her student government. She supervises the student government committee that distributes funds to clubs and campus organizations. Claire has been considering proposing a resolution to limit the amount of funding a single club can receive, and recently noticed that one particular club files a lot of funding requests and receives consistent approval. While the club makes good use of all the money it is allocated, other clubs with equal needs receive significantly less. Claire knows that Garret, the head of the student government's funding committee, is also the club's president. Garrett is an excellent member of student government. He helped streamline the funding process, dedicated his year to making better forms, and supported clubs with better how-to guides for the process.

Garrett makes no effort to hide or minimize his participation in the club, and Claire does not believe he intentionally approves more proposals submitted by his club. When Claire speaks to Garret, it is obvious that he feels he is entirely neutral in the process. He even abstains from the vote when his own club's proposals are raised. Still, Claire wonders if she should continue to allow his committee to approve requests for his club. The other members of the committee admire Garrett, who is their leader, and are likely to trust any proposal submitted by his group because it is associated with him. Since he helps craft proposals, they are already exceptional in comparison to submissions by less experienced and knowledgeable clubs.

Claire also considers putting a spending cap on individual clubs, but worries the constraint will limit creative ideas. It could also personally insult Garrett, and she does not want to derail his excellent work. Claire feels something must be done to make the system more fair, but she is unsure what, if anything, will work.

What would you do in Claire's position? Do you think Garrett's committee can continue to approve his club's proposals? Can Garrett's situation be called a conflict of interest? How does his position give the club an advantage? Can the club fairly benefit from the advantage, particularly if it is unintentional? Should upper-level members of student government be allowed to service in leadership roles for other student organizations or clubs?

Student funding is by far one of the most important and interesting topics student leaders are confronted with. The answers to the unending questions about funding varies from institution to institution. There are a few systems, however, that can come into play that empower student leaders and student groups to make reaching those answers a little easier. For example, at our university, a student financial auditing system was in the process of being created to prevent financial spending, reporting, and allocation abuses. As much as it was reactive, what was most important was its prevention of financially dishonest practices. It was an initiative spearheaded by the student government, fellow student leaders, and even a few professors.

Creating systems that both prevent and address overarching concerns allows you and your organization to keep the health, sustainability, and integrity of your work intact.

Scenario 5: Social Media Struggle

In the last few weeks, Matt, a student government senator, has started to see a lot of videos on social media showing students drinking alcohol and challenging their friends to do the same. When Matt logged into his Facebook this morning, he noticed a video of John, one of his fellow senators, had been posted. John is not 21, and in the video, he is wearing his student government sweatshirt as he chugs several beers. Matt works hard to follow the rules and always represent student government professionally, and he feels that John has done a disservice to the organization. John is a very popular and an effective student leader. John's Facebook is also set to private, so only his friends will see the video.

Matt is afraid that if he comes forward, he'll be blamed by other senators for telling on John, and excluded from the organization's sense of camaraderie. He also feels what John has done is unprofessional and poorly represents the organization. Matt is torn.

What should Matt do? How do social media posts affect a person's professionalism or standing within an organization? Would your reaction be different if John were not wearing student government apparel? Does your student government have any regulations related to social media activity? Warren Buffett said, "It takes twenty years to build a reputation and five minutes to ruin it. If you think about that, you'll do things differently." Stories like Matt's and John's are not unfamiliar or unheard of in student leadership, let alone in college.

What you choose to do is your choice alone. What can be tricky, however, is when the mentality of "my choice" has the power to negatively impact the mission of "our organization." Enjoying yourself in school and having fun are definitely things you want to have during your college experience. When you choose to portray yourself in a particular light, also consider other choices you have made or are about to make. Are they contradictory? Do they align?

All's Well that Ends Well

By now it's clear your role in student leadership comes with some tough decisions as well as a title. There are times when leaders are torn in making decisions that always satisfy the popular opinion versus making a decision they feel is in the best interest of their constituents. Keep in mind that for every choice you make, there are tenfold who are affected by it. Keep yourself accountable to your mission, and to what you stand for. As a student leader you get the privilege of sitting at tables with individuals who have a say on what happens at the university. Your goal should always consist of keeping in mind those who are not at the table with you. What would they say? What are their needs? Their concerns?

The hope and goal of this chapter is to get you to ask questions that place you in the best possible position, especially when it comes to representing others. You have the power and the position to make certain choices others do not. What are you going to do with this power?

KEY CONCEPTS

1. Do not be afraid to ask for help from a mentor, advisor, or peer.

2. Different institutions and organizations value different things. What does your institution value?

3. Sometimes what is right may not be fair, and what may be fair can be seen as wrong. Have the necessary conversations to work through things.

4. Being a student leader is a constant learning process. Uphold your mission, vision, and values to the best of your ability.

MY REFLECTION

ZOE JIMENEZ | RESIDENT ASSISTANT
UNIVERSITY OF NOTRE DAME

I was part of a student coalition to gain a gay-straight alliance organization at the University of Notre Dame. We were successful due to the efforts of the leaders, one of whom became the student body president of Notre Dame and later, a Rhodes scholar. In my senior year at Notre Dame, I was a Resident Assistant of Breen-Phillips Hall and a resource to any minority or queer women in the dorm. Through this job, I met with administrators who shared my vision of creating a more inclusive campus for gender and sexual minority students. With them, I served on an administrative committee to discuss the campus environment for these students and discuss ways in which the university could improve. At the end of my senior year, I created the Transgender Ally Program with the Gender Relations Center of Notre Dame.

Having firsthand experience with student body governments that both shied away from and rose to the challenge of complicated moral situations. I can relate to being faced with representing a university with whom I did not share the same values. My moral dilemmas came from reconciling my personal beliefs with the duty I had to represent a University who did not completely understand a sizeable portion of the students who attended it. As a resident assistant, I was asked to encourage my residents to attend Catholic mass at our residential chapel, while knowing that many of the students with whom I counseled did not share the same beliefs.

Similarly, as a representative of the university, I was also asked to represent the moral teaching of the Catholic Church. For the most part, this was easy, as I was exposed to Catholicism since I was 3 years old. However, through my work with the coalition for a gay-straight alliance, I had made friends who identified as transgender. The Catholic Church does not formally recognize the struggle of these individuals so I could not offer direct support to them, but knowing how dire the state of affairs is for transgender individuals, I felt this was not something I could compromise, personally, morally, and ethically.

Since I could not offer support officially through the dorm I served, I reached out to the Gender Relations Center of Notre Dame and asked if they would be willing to collaborate on the creation of a theologically-compatible transgender ally educational program. I was faced with a difficult and ethical situation but at the end of the day, I made a choice to stand up for what I believed.

8. POWER AND INFLUENCE
KAREEM AREF|FORMER PRESIDENT
UNIVERSITY OF CALIFORNIA STUDENT ASSOCIATION

Whether you are newly elected or appointed, by virtue of your position, how much power do you think you have? To command real power, you'll need to understand the concepts of power and influence along with the difference between the two. Power is most simply defined as "the ability to make something happen that otherwise would not have." Influence, is the ability to empower another person to utilize their power in order to make something happen. Before discussing these concepts any further, it is important to realize several basic truths of power.

Where is Power?

First and foremost, Power is everywhere and nowhere. While this may sound abstract and amorphous it is actually quite simple. In every interaction power is exchanged. By virtue of being an autonomous human being you have a baseline of power. This base power stems from the way in which you carry yourself, the words you choose to represent your thoughts, the company you keep, and the respect you command. Our baseline power level is essentially a derivative of our own personal characteristics and how we use or represent those traits in our daily lives. While power does vary from person to person, there is no reason that your own traits cannot make you as powerful as someone else with different traits. Your power stems from within you, existing nowhere until you command it to arise and is constantly in a state of flux.

From the first moment of any interaction, regardless of context, power and influence is being traded. When approaching another individual to engage in conversation you are attempting to exert power to create the conversation you desire. When a handshake takes place, there are inherent undertones of the powers that the individuals are exchanging. These exchanges occur when transferring power from one person to another, allowing power to exist everywhere.

The second major truth about power is that we have the ability to control our power and its subsequent impacts. Throughout my term as Vice President of External Affairs at the University of California, Riverside, I made it a point to state in each meeting that "we are powerful." My colleagues remember this fondly and it is important to realize the significance of the statement was far more than that of a mere catchphrase. We are powerful because we each have our own agency and desires which we can use to make things happen. The key to this truth is understanding that the only barrier between you and your power is the limits you place on yourself. Where there is a will, there is a way, simple as that. In order to be in control of your power you must reflect on it, especially as a student leader.

Much like many cartoons and television programs, in order to control your power, you must understand its source. Your source of power does not come from a magic wand nor does it stem from an all-powerful ring. Your power is a product of you and as such you must reflect on who you are in order to find your strength and your voice. Each personality type and trait must be tapped into differently and it is important to understand your personality traits and what your strengths are as a leader.

Finding Your Source of Power

Do you have the ability to speak well with others? Are you there for people when they need you? Are you an accepting, open-minded and inclusive person? Do people seek out your wisdom and consul by coming to you for advice? Find your inner strengths and use them to amplify your power and influence. While we are powerful, alone you are powerless. The President of the United States is viewed as the most powerful person in the world, but if they had no United States behind them, they would be powerless. Just as we exchange power between one another we must understand that without others, power does not exist. This concept is especially lucid in terms of government. The President may control the country, but without the people's support, The President would have no power to run the country with. If the leader is not in power, the people will be forced to go without the basic comforts that "civilized society" offers. It does not matter how powerful you are, because without those around you,

you are nothing. This idea has been a constant reminder for me to remain humble regardless of what position I hold. You are not better than anyone else by virtue of your power.

Remember that powerful people do not put others down, they lift them up. Powerful people share their power and empower others to achieve their goals.

This basic framework can be used to understand power. Power is constantly stemming from one individual to another. It only comes to life based on those who have the ability to control power. As a student leader, you have been entrusted by your constituents to hold a greater source of power.

Power is your ability to make something happen and influence allows you to make other people use their power, but with the power you have been endowed, a simple question is posed: Is power a good thing?

It allows us to get what we want and to ensure that our will is being followed. Who are we to believe that our will alone should be acted upon? Is power a bad thing? In the wrong hands history has shown us the tragic and horrendous things that come from misplaced power. In order to end these horrible events someone of equal or greater power had to step forward. So is power inherently good or bad?

Neither. Power is neither objectively positive nor negative. Power is only a reflection of its wielder. It is not inherently negative to be powerful. In fact, being powerful can be a great thing. It makes us feel confident about our actions and abilities while allowing us to enact change to benefit our constituents. Never forget why you have your power. Your power as a leader is entrusted to you in order to allow you to benefit your constituents. We have all heard about it before, powerful people appointing their friends or family to high level positions. These scandals occur because the person in power has forgotten why they were given the power in the first place. Do not be that person! Just as you have to reflect on your own source of personal power, you must also bear in mind where you draw your power from. Your power is essentially a loan from your supporters to use their collective voices to accomplish something greater than anyone thought possible. Keeping in mind the source of your power and why you wield it will allow you to guide your actions on the correct path rather than stray away.

Utilizing Your Power

Power can be used in many ways, but there are two primary methods with examples listed below. Keep in mind, positive and negative are not being used as normative, but rather as an affirmative act or negation in the following paragraph.

Exerting Power over Others

Chris is the student leader and he never listens to his Vice President. Each time his VP brings an idea to the table; Chris is quick to shut it down and reminds his VP who the President of the organization is.

This happens quite often. You could easily tell when you have a student leader who is power hungry if they are acting like this.

Power Exerted Over You

Jessica is the Vice Chair of her organization, and has a monthly meeting with her Executive Director. The Executive Director for her organization, a professional staff member, handles the organization's logistics and acts as an advisor. During a hot discussion regarding budgets, the Executive Director tries to convince Jessica about a certain decision and reminds her of the many years of experience he has and why she should vote against it.

While it is important for Jessica to listen to her Executive Director, she is obligated to do what is best for her constituents. Your sound judgment, qualifications, and thoughtful reasoning, are part of the reasons why you are in your position. Do not doubt yourself.

When to Use Power

When deciding what methods to use, a leader must decide what is more important to them. Factors like respect and honor or fear and obedience. Either choice could be reached by a reasonable person, but ruling with respect and honor is typically the far better choice for utilizing power. Respect and honor are well received by those you serve and often translate to an easier path in the long run, though the short term changes will often be more difficult. Fear and obedience are often looked to as a sure fire mode of control. Despite this belief, one must be immensely powerful in order to be feared. Once the populous is sick of you, history tells us that you will likely end up in less than comfortable circumstances.

When holding an elected position as a student representative it is important to remember that you are performing a service. Your title gives you power, but that does not and should not result in you commanding those who are in the fight with you. Every time you use your power in a way that is poorly received, your influence will decrease until you are ultimately given no credibility. Utilizing power must not diminish the respect others have for your work, or else you will not be in power for long.

Allowing others to exercise power over you is an alternative approach to using power. Our power is not diminished by allowing another person to take control of the situation. In fact, your power as a leader can often be increased by following under another leader. This allows your work to gain influence over those who you have worked for. Usually elected officials are not the primary force behind the legislative bills that they introduce.

Oftentimes, it is their staffers who are authoring policy. This is because these individuals allow themselves to work for another's cause. Their dedication builds trust and gives them influence over the primary power holder.

My father used to tell me that you have two ears and one mouth, so you must listen twice as much as you speak. Unfortunately, we are too often swept away in a moment, feeling that we must act immediately. This is not the most effective use of your power and, often times, this can lead to lost effort. The most powerful leaders are those whom everyone listens to carefully when they speak. For you to attain this stature, listen carefully to others, methodically form your opinion, and speak only when you believe your words will have an impact.

This method essentially focuses your power into a concise and powerful statement that others will remember. It is important to recognize that power and influence is an exchange between individuals which occurs every day.

While the use of power can be focused on gaining more power and creating change, we must all come to terms with the fact that our power will not last forever. A true leader cultivates new leaders and, as such, must not only attempt to attain power, but also to give power. As student leaders, we may have a couple years to work at full capacity and if we do not pass on our knowledge and power we will have accomplished nothing. It is easy to get swept up in the moment and feel important. It is human nature to want to be in charge and feel needed, but in order to be a true leader you must ensure that your infrastructure and mentees are able to take on your power.

Student government offices, and offices in general, each serve a purpose. In order to achieve that purpose, those in the office must not only be powerful in their own right, but also have a strong infrastructure that supports that power. When you have taken office, look closely at your mission statement and develop a system that will help you to best execute this. When I served as the Vice President of External Affairs, I realized the office had 3 main goals centering on legislation, organizing, and engagement. Once I had identified these aspects, I rewrote my bylaws in order to ensure each office was properly staffed by a director and several directors who were more specialized. Each branch also had a committee under it. I expanded the office to over 100 students.

When taking on this kind of expansion, in order to capitalize on the power of the members you must remember that each person in this group plays an integral part. Enshrining this system within a written bylaw will allow those who come after you to get right to work rather than having to restructure.

In any office with each change in level your power decreases, as such ensure that you only create those positions necessary to support the main goal and try not to remove yourself from the process. Once an infrastructure is in place to allow power to be carried on for future generations you must understand that holding all the power does a disservice to your constituents. You must spread the wealth. If you have gathered power, it is your duty to pass that on to the younger generation so they might advance the mission of your office once you are gone. It is essential that you are selfless in your use of power. Give authority to those around you, and allow them the opportunity to succeed and organize by your side. Power is ultimately worthless if it is not used to empower others.

Just as our power as elected representatives stems from the people, it is essential that you use that power in turn to energize and invigorate those on the ground floor of the cause. You must master this basic understanding of what power is in order to use it and when using it you must understand the ramifications of your actions. Never forget that without a strong foundation even the tallest mountain will fall. As such you must establish a strong infrastructure and group to continue the fight to build towards the end goal.

KEY CONCEPTS

1. Power is the ability to make "things" happen that otherwise would not.

2. Influence is the ability to get others to use their power to create change.

3. Power is constantly being created from within you and exchanged with those around you. As a student leader, it is alright to allow other student leaders to command that power in order to encourage future generation to step up.

4. Power is neither bad nor good simply a reflection of those who wield it.

5. Power must be used with its effects on others in mind.

6. To be successful your power must be shared and supported.

MY REFLECTION

JOURDAN HILAIRE, M. ED|FORMER PRESIDENT OF A.P.A.C.
CALIFORNIA STATE UNIVERSITY, FULLERTON

T.E.A.M. has been the driving force of my leadership style since 2011. I was born and raised in Los Angeles, California and earned my bachelor's degree from California State University, Fullerton. While attending CSUF, I was elected and served as the President of Alliance for the Preservation of African Consciousness (A.P.A.C.) from the summer of 2011 to May 2013. A.P.A.C's main goal is to provide unity among Black males on campus, and to promote the consciousness of our African American history of yesterday and today. There's no power and influence without a team. Power and influence within a team has the ability to accomplish goals when utilized correctly. Being elected president of A.P.A.C was my first leadership role in which I had the opportunity to inspire change and create structure. My first semester in that role was the toughest because I was not exactly sure how to use my newly attained power. In my first semester as the president, I did not understand the concept of T.E.A.M. or how to manage a team to accomplish goals. I conducted myself as a "one-man show" and utilized the members of the organization as helpers rather than partners. Decisions were forced instead of opinions and new ideas flowing in meetings. The following semester I had a chat with one of my mentors.

He mentioned, "use your team before you lose your team. Empower them to make decisions. You cannot be president and do it all. In everything you do in A.P.A.C. never forget, Together Everyone Achieves More (T.E.A.M)."

Shortly after that conversation, I had a meeting with my team and apologized for my actions and reassured them that together we will achieve more. Leading up to my second year as president, we were able to plan programs, participate in community service, and participate in a few team barbecues to build brotherhood. Now, when I think about power and influence, I think about responsibility, empowerment, and T.E.A.M. Always remember, there's no power without support.

9. SETTING REALISTIC GOALS
ROHULLAH LATIF| FORMER STUDENT BODY PRESIDENT
CSU FULLERTON

Society's mightiest heroes did not just wake up one day and accomplish something great. They set goals along their journeys and worked tirelessly to accomplish them. This same mentality can be applied to a student leader. Before you start your position or find out about an open position, do your research. Here are two examples of what could happen if you do not set proper goals and do not conduct a thorough research.

Goal Setting Example #1

It was the day before the deadline for applications for student government president, when Anna decided to submit her application. Everyone was excited for her to be running and clearly she was the favorite amongst the other candidates, one of them being Jessica. Then it came time for the "friendly debate" which was televised live on local TV. The broadcast attracted a record breaking number of students to the university auditorium. Immediately, you could tell that Jessica and the other candidates were more knowledgeable on the topics than Anna was. The simplest questions about the university baffled Anna, while everyone else answered with ease. Students started whispering and many of them lost their confidence in Anna.

Jessica and the other candidates spent hours upon hours studying the history of the university. They reviewed everything from student bills, to legislations, and even the origins of the university. Meanwhile, Anna was out partying, thinking she will win the election based solely off her popularity. She got arrogant and failed to do basic research that would have aided her in the debate. The election results came in and Jessica won the election by a landslide.

Goal Setting Example #2

Adam is interviewing for the "Environmental Leader" position. He is extremely qualified, has been involved in community service, has a stellar GPA, and is an all-around outstanding person. During his interview, Adam mentioned his ideas are innovative and have not been tried before. He spoke about how he wanted to get rid of plastic bags on campus and to change the bylaws to add a Vice President position. Adam soon realized that Roy, one of the interviewers, was the current Environmental Leader.

Adam did not know this, but Roy was finalizing the agenda to approve a new Vice President. Roy had also collected and submitted a ticket for the upcoming election so students could vote on the plastic bag issue. Most of his talking points were already in progress by the current Environmental Leader, yet Adam had no clue. Needless to say, Adam did not pass the 1st interview.

How to Prepare

First off, when applying to any position, make sure you conduct a thorough research. Find out who was in that position at least 2 years prior and understand their priorities. Find out what their goals were, what they were able to accomplish, and what prior and on-going projects and initiatives were important during that time. Understanding some of the road blocks leaders before you faced can help you pick up some of their unfinished work. Be proactive about reaching out and learning from that person in the short time you have between your election/appointment and their transition. Obtaining information from students, who have already experienced what you are preparing for, is invaluable. If that person is still around school, find them and see if you can pick their brain over coffee.

So you found some information about that position. Great! Now you are ready to come up with your own goals! Write all of your original ideas. Anything! Let it flow. For each plan you write mention the following and also make sure to develop a concrete action plan. You can develop an action plan by answering the following questions:

Why is it important to you?

What is it that truly drives and motivates you about student government? Why do you choose to participate in student government? What do you want to see changed and how can it help your constituents?

How can you achieve it?

Now that you have figured out 3-4 important topics, you can come up with an action plan. Take as much time as you need to come up with a proper action plan for each of your goals. People will follow you if you can give them a CONCRETE ACTION PLAN instead of empty promises. An action is only effective if you attach a solid deadline to it. By developing a timeline people will begin to realize you have really put a lot of thought into this goal and are determined to achieve it. I won my election by providing concrete goals, timelines, and methods of funding my goals.

From Preparation to Action

Every weekend, my running mate and I were in the library for hours in front of a white board hashing out the issues and developing our agenda and concrete action plans. Finally, we decided to tackle issues regarding communication, outreach, sustainability, unity, and a few more. Below I have listed something I like to call "fluff goals." These are goals that do not have any backing to them and instead seem like false promises. Do not, I repeat, do not develop goals similar to these. Below you will first find a "fluff goal" followed by a realistic goal.

"In order to be an effective student government, we will do whatever it takes to regularly hear from our constituents."

So you will do whatever it takes? What does that even mean? For a student who is a commuter, or a parent that rarely comes to school, how can you relate to them? With the goal above, you really cannot. Instead of that fluff above, try expressing your goals with concrete action plans. A better example of the above fluff goal can be the following:

In order to effectively listen to our constituents, we will hold office hours every day of the week in different locations to better accommodate the schedule of our students.

Do you see the difference? The first one was fluff the second one was a concrete action plan.

"We will educate and empower students to make this campus a better place for everyone."

That all sounds great, but someone will always ask you how you will do that? It is better to have that answer incorporated with your original statement like the statement below:

We want to educate and motivate our students by providing the campus with three (3) workshops a semester; workshops such as Alcohol Awareness, Stress Management, and Financial Literacy.

By providing students the tools they will obtain from these workshops, you are actually empowering them and making the campus a better place.

"We will also focus our efforts in revamping our communication and

marketing efforts for our events."

My running mate and I personally faced this one during our campaign. We had to come up with a solution to remedy our overall communication issue on campus. To our luck we met a student who was sitting outside the math building (on the east side of the campus), alone, eating his sandwich. I asked him if he knew about the other events that were happening on campus (west). He responded with "no, but I wish there was a way to know about the events on this side of the campus (east)." At that moment, an idea popped in my head. What if we put up a large electronic display board on the building right in front of us? We decided to go with it and converted that valuable encounter into a realistic goal as shown below:

We will increase communication on campus by installing an electronic display board on the financial aid building so students from the east side of the campus are also aware of the events taking place on campus.

Improving campus communication is always a hot agenda item during elections. They key is always to set yourself apart from everyone else.

"We will reduce parking fees by $100."

Be careful with making false promises. At least at my school, our parking department was a separate organization, one which I had no direct power over.

Saying you will reduce the price by $100 will be stretching it unless you have proof. As a student I had no idea why our parking permits were so expensive. It was not until I sat down with the Director of Parking & Transportation, that I realized our parking department offers so much to the campus. They provided free bus passes, car rentals, started a bike loan program, built a new parking structure to alleviate parking congestion, provided free bike checkups, and so much more. Instead of making risky promise, try this below:

> *"We will fight on your behalf to ensure that any increases to our parking permits are placed on a ballot for you to vote on."*

This displays a sign of transparency and proper representation. If the school wants to build another parking structure and increase the parking fees, then you will ensure that it is placed on the ballot for students to vote on. Whatever the outcome, your promise to your constituents is to represent their voice and a vote on a ballot will help you do that. If the students vote yes, then great everything goes through. If they vote no, then it becomes your responsibility to represent your students.

After you get the hang of it, it will become easier to understand. Student government is like reality television. You are not really famous and everyone forgets about you in the end if you do not stand out. The best way to stand out from your competition, is by having a detailed plan. The more you provide, the more people will have a reason to believe in you.

Improving the Goals, Never Settle for Average

Now that you have developed your goals, use your resources to gather some feedback about them. Gather some of your closest allies and ask them to go through your plans. Encourage them to ask you questions and be ready to defend your answers. This will help prepare you for any upcoming debates and or Q&A sessions. If you are running in an election, make sure to present to as many clubs and organization as possible. Fast-forward to the day you have either been appointed or elected to a position. Take a few days off and go celebrate, you have earned it!

Once you are back, it is time to get to work. It is essential that you start to work on your goals as soon as you can. The year will go by quickly.

In order to make any sort of substantial change on your campus, you have to make the most of your time. Do not be that leader who unsuccessfully tries to scramble at the end of their term, because they are trying to accomplish unrealistic or poorly executed goals. Your platform is your commitment to your students and constituents. Sometimes you realize that your previous goals and what you promised in the beginning is no longer achievable. It could be due to budget cuts or other issues that no one could have foreseen. If that happens, it is important to stay flexible and understanding of the situation. That does not mean you give up on your idea, it means you hit the drawing board again and figure out how you can still accomplish your goal.

During my term I had made a few promises. One was to develop an actual five-year strategic plan for the entire student government; a process that took 6 months to complete, with over 120 people, who participated and provided feedback. Another promise was an electronic display board. Not only did I have to convince the students to invest $110,000 into purchasing this display board, I had to convince the university to pitch in approximately $40,000 to paint the building where this board was going up. That goal took my entire 1-year term to complete. It required many meetings, late nights, and proper planning. Any idea you have will sound great in your head and to others, but in reality it will be a lot more difficult to execute. Remember, there are rules, regulations, winning others over, and many other factors that will get in your way. Keep pushing and fighting for your goals. I was able to keep all my promises, will you?

KEY CONCEPTS

1. Set goals in all facets and at all levels of your life. Whether it's a short term personal goal or long-term professional goals, make sure you have a plan with defined outcomes to motivate you and keep you on track.

2. People will follow leaders who have strong, concrete action plans as part of their goals.

3. Develop strong goals by answering the following:

   a. Why is it important to you?
   b. How can you achieve it?
   c. What is your timeline?

4. Present your goals and concrete action plans to your closest allies and listen to their opinions and thoughts.

5. Any goal you put on a flyer or present in public becomes a promise you make to your constituents.

MY REFLECTION

DANNY O' DONOVAN | STUDENT UNION PRESIDENT
CORK INSTITUTE OF TECHNOLOGY, IRELAND

Even across the Atlantic Ocean, setting realistic goals is no less important in the situation of an Irish Student Government organization. We too recognize the importance of the time taken to sharpen the axe, prior to going for the tree. In Ireland, higher education is part of the public sector, a sector which in some areas is understaffed, underfunded, and where sometimes there is very little incentive given for improvement. This makes the role of the student leader even more challenging in setting goals that can be achieved within the timeframe of their elected term.

One quickly realizes the importance of the word "realistic" for a plethora of reasons. The first and most important is that no student leader operates in a bubble. Not only do student leaders have teams that they will have to manage, but they will also have to negotiate and work with various levels of other staff and management within the university. Goals are usually intrinsically driven; thus it will be hard to instill the same passion in someone else to help achieve a goal that you have identified. One of the key considerations in doing so is making sure that your goal has a universal appeal. This may mean slightly re-considering your initial goal, but the more people that can get behind it, the greater the possibility of it reaching fruition.

Time is one of the biggest hurdles to the achievement of any student leader's goals. Firstly, you are operating in a finite term, where every second counts, yet every second of the day seems to be filled with unforeseen tasks, which can have one feeling like they are permanently "firefighting." It is important to recognize the scale of the time constraints at play, in setting goals that are realistic. I would recommend setting aside time to work on long-term strategic goals every week, otherwise one will be stuck a loop of constant firefighting.

Additionally the members of staff and university administration, who will be key in enabling the achievement of your goals seem to have all the time in the world. They are more than likely in a permanent, 9-5 positions. Thus you will find that you are both working off different timescales and levels of urgency. You may have a great idea that is one hundred percent feasible, but can be a difficult deliverable within your term. Succession planning and ensuring continuity is key to overcoming this. Though you cannot influence who gets elected as your successor, ensuring a good crossover of your work and a solid introduction to staff can do wonders for their chances of realizing your goals long after you have moved on.

10. GENERAL MEETINGS
ROHULLAH LATIF | FORMER STUDENT BODY PRESIDENT
CSU FULLERTON

Meetings can be either the most or least productive part of your day. I do not think there is anything more frustrating that attending meetings where nothing gets done all the while you have a million other things you could be doing. People talking over others, the chair not controlling the meeting, and just absolute chaos. I can almost guarantee; you will be in one of these meetings at one point in your life if you have not already been in one. As a leader it is essential you know how to facilitate your own meetings and understand how to behave during meetings.

How to Run Meetings
Every elected leader needs to learn how to run meetings. Fortunately, I had previous experience with facilitating meetings before my term as Student Body President. Every meeting should have a purpose and be as timely and efficient as possible. Meetings with structure and format will typically accomplish more than meetings without.

Meeting Agenda
Always develop a meeting agenda at least 72 hours before your meeting. This will give you ample time to distribute the agenda to all the members attending. Depending on the state you live in, distributing the agenda 72 hours in advance is also law if your organization is incorporated.

Everyone should have enough time to review the items, and come prepared for the meeting. By distributing the agenda in advance you now put the responsibility for being prepared on the members of your organization.

Keep minutes

No matter what kind of meeting you are in, always take some sort of meeting minutes (notes). Having minutes is a great way to remember what you discussed and ensure there are tangible takeaways from general discussions. Below are a few tips to help you take minutes.

- Always keep track of the location, time, and date of the meeting.
- Keep track of who is at the meeting, who is late, and who did not show up.
- Be prepared! Make sure you have all the necessary note-taking utensils you need before the meeting.
- Use the restroom before the meeting. There is nothing worse than needing to go to the restroom during an important discussion.
- Be completely neutral and keep your writing clear and concise. Minutes are legal documents so make sure you are writing accurately.
- Appoint a person dedicated to only taking minutes during the meeting. It's not good practice to chair a meeting and also take minutes.
- Lastly, have your minutes reviewed by a few other people before it becomes an official document.

Time

When I was President of the Inter-Fraternity Council (President of all the fraternities), my meetings would start at 4 pm on Tuesdays. There would always be a few members who would show up late. The meeting would be scheduled for 4 pm, but I would have to start the meeting at 4:20 pm because I was waiting for everyone.

Half way through the semester we were voting on a controversial item and I had enough of everyone coming in late. As the clock hit 4 pm, I started the meeting. I barely had quorum (the minimum number of members required to start meetings), but continued the meeting, discussed, and voted on the item. Fifteen minutes later 2 other voting members showed up. During the meeting one of them said the following:

Voting Member: "Excuse me, but some of us never got a chance to vote on the item that just passed, that is not fair!"

Me: "Can I ask you a question?"

Voting member: "Sure"

Me: "Your chapter elected you to attend these meetings right? What time does this meeting start?"

Voting Member: "4 pm!"

Me: "What time is it?"

Voting Member: "umm... 4:25 pm."

Me: "If you want your chapter to have a voice on the matter, please make the effort to show up on time."

I had to be stern, or they were not going to take me seriously. After that meeting, for the rest of the semester, everyone was on time. If you say you are going to start a meeting at 4pm, start the meeting exactly on time. Do not wait around and allow people to come late. Although I faced some backlash because it was a controversial item, I had to maintain my grounds for the sake of order.

Roberts Rule of Order

If you have not already, you need to pick up a book or Google basic rules to Robert's Rule of Order if you have not been trained on the subject matter yet.

Robert's Rules of Order is the standard for meetings. It is a way of conducting meetings using parliamentary procedure. Understanding this complex method can help you successfully chair meetings. So invest in Robert's Rules of Order and actively use its methods. Ideally, Robert's Rules of Order provide a method for meetings to be run efficiently. Much like a chess game, however, if you do not know the rules, the meeting can become daunting and those who understand the rules can control the meeting. In order to ensure you can contribute effectively take the time to learn the rules, understand that they are designed to facilitate your ability to be heard, and help those around you to gain sufficient understanding. One of the most essential tactics I took away from Robert's Rules of Order is to never let two people speak at once. Nothing is set in stone yet. Just because there is an agenda in front of you does not mean it will pass.

Keep that in mind, any report or agenda is merely a recommendation just as any rule or bylaw can be changed, suspended, or deleted.

There should always be one person talking while others are placed on a speakers list. There should always be a speakers list. This allows everyone an opportunity to speak once first before moving to the second speaker list. After everyone has finished speaking one time, the chair can then open up the second speakers list for people who want to speak again. Above all, you cannot just speak and blurt out whatever is on your mind. You have to be recognized by the chairperson before you can speak. Anytime you do speak, direct it to the chair of the meeting.

Ideally, this limits personal attacks among board members. Make sure to use proper language when addressing other members or the chairperson. Below are some tips, tricks, and terms that will help you grasp the basics of Robert's Rules of Order.

Point of Information
Suppose you are discussing the possibility of funding a spring concert. While in a heated discussion, you did not hear how many people are estimated to attend the event and you want that information repeated again. You could then say "Point of Information" and then be able to ask your question. This is used to ask a question or clarify a point.

Point of Order

If someone speaks out of turn or starts talking about items not on the agenda. You must say "Point of Order" immediately after the individual's infraction. The Chair will then bring everything back to the agenda item. This is a common occurrence.

Divide the Question

This is pretty neat and allows you to divide a motion into two separate motions. For example, if there is a motion on the floor that is too complicated, or has multiple parts, then you use this technique to make the voting less confusing. It can also be used to allow those who agree with part, but not all of the motion on the floor to be heard.

Move to Amend

You can amend any motion on the floor by saying "I wish to amend…" This is one of the most important techniques to understand.

Consider an agenda item is being discussed in a meeting. Angelica addresses the chair, is recognized, and makes the following motion:

Angelica: "I move to buy a printer and scanner." This is seconded by another member.
Chair: "It is moved to buy a printer and scanner. Is there any discussion?" Jackie wants to make an amendment, so she addresses the chair, is recognized and makes her amendment to the motion.

Jackie: "I move to amend the motion by adding at the end not to exceed the cost of $1000." This is then seconded by another member.

Chair: "It is moved and seconded to amend the motion by adding at the end not to exceed the cost of $1000. If amended, the motion would read to buy a printer and scanner, not to exceed the cost of $1000. Is there any discussion on the amendment." Then another member wants to amend the amendment.

Dennis: "I move to amend the amendment by striking out $1000 and inserting $2000." This is seconded by another member.

Chair: "It is moved and seconded to amend the amendment by striking out $1000 and inserting $2000. If amended, it would read not to exceed the cost of $2000. Is there any discussion on the amendment?"

The discussion would be limited to discussing $1000 vs $2000. Further amendments would be out of order until these two amendments are voted on. The chair would first start by having a discussion on the last amendment which was to strike out $1000. The board would then vote on whether they think they should keep $1000 or $2000 and make their way back down to the original motion.

Postpone to a Certain Time

You can use this technique if you feel that there is not enough information presented. Once you motion to postpone the agenda items, be sure to provide a detailed description of why you are postponing it and to what date. This would need a second and a vote.

Reconsider

Jess makes an amendment or motion and it passes. Let's say Jess changes her mind later on in the meeting about how she feels about her previous vote. She could then reconsider her vote. Only the people who voted for the motion can bring the motion back on the agenda for reconsideration. The rules dictate that a motion may only be reconsidered after a significant amount of time has elapsed and this usually takes place in a different meeting.

Hear Everyone's Input

There are many different personalities present during meetings. Not everyone will have the courage to raise their hand and speak. As a leader, it is important for you to have the input of everyone in the room. If you are discussing an election between two people and 4/5 people in the meeting have given their input, then you should pause and ask the 5th person what they think. Sometimes the quiet ones have the best ideas. Next time you are chairing a meeting, make sure you hear everyone talk at least once about each agenda item. If you do not, feel free to call on them to hear their input.

Different Personalities

Understanding the different personalities will help you run successful meetings. Throughout my career as a student leader, I had been fortunate enough to run numerous meetings which exposed me different personalities early on. Learning to identify these personalities will help you greatly during your term.

The Negative One

This person is always negative. They will have nothing positive to say and tend to bring down any idea or thought presented at the meeting. You need to be careful with this person. People will be afraid to express their thoughts because they fear the negative one attacking their view. They can be categorized as a pessimist, which is not necessarily a bad personality type to have in your group.

"If everyone in your team agrees with you, then something is wrong with your team."

Having said that, there is a fine line between unnecessary negativity and providing counter arguments to flesh out an idea. So tread across those lines very carefully. Make sure you are acknowledging this person when they speak and hear them out. They are so used to people shutting them off completely that it might surprise them when someone actually listens to them.

The Shy One

This person is extremely shy. They will talk, but only if

given the opportunity. The shy one will sometimes have great ideas so make sure you ask for their point of view. Your job is not to crack them out of their shells, but to respect their personality.

During one of my previous student leadership, I encountered this type of a leader. I tried and tried to involve her and even made her chair the meeting in front of 25 people. This was a bad idea, because I was forcing her to do something she was not comfortable doing and so she fainted. Yes…fainted! Some people are not as comfortable or as extroverted as you may be, and you need to understand and respect that fact.

Peanut Butter and Jelly

This represents two people who are always on the same page and are constantly whispering and talking during meetings. Any time one says something, the other backs them up, and if one disagrees so does the other. This can become really annoying, causing cliques to form, and ultimately affects the entire team. Personally, I handled this situation, by strategically separating them. Before the meeting, I removed the extra chairs and had everyone purposely sit in different seats. I also had a meeting with each one of them privately. During the meeting I expressed the following:

"During meetings it is important to be respectful of everyone's time. I really feel distracted when you two whisper and talk amongst yourself. That's the main reason why I separated you. I would really appreciate it if you two could please stop whispering to each other during our meetings."

Something as simple as that could really make a difference. It is often not as effective to directly call them out or tell them to "please shut up" during the meeting. That will just cause more problems down the line. It is better to pull them aside and talk to them privately.

The Talkative One

This person will not stop talking and loves expressing how they feel about every agenda item. They will forget what they are talking about and can easily go off topic. First, pull them aside and speak to them privately. If that does not work, then as chair you need to cut them off if they continue to speak too much or simply not recognize them.

If you choose to cut them off, please do so in a respectful manner. Below is an example of a meeting where all the personalities are present.

Jessica is chairing a 10-person meeting. There are many different personalities in this meeting. There is Adam, who is a Negative Nancy, Karen, who is extremely shy, Laura and Kim, who are always on the same page, and Daren, who is controlling and loves talking. The chair opens up the meeting. Someone motions to speak about approving the snow day event and it's open for discussion. Daren talks first.

Daren: "I just love this idea. I think we should definitely follow through with this. I mean, come on, no one has ever done this on campus before. We could be the first and become legends on campus. Everyone loves snow, I mean, I know the snow is not going to be as great or real but heck it is still snow. Actually, last time I saw snow was when I was 12 years old in Colorado…"

Chair: "Point of order Daren. Thank you for your input. Please stay on the issue at hand, which is approving the snow day event. I appreciate your enthusiasm, but we can't go off track. Who hasn't spoken that wants to speak?"

Adam: "I think this is a terrible idea. Daren we live near

Big Bear Mountain where it snows! I am sure everyone has seen snow. We shouldn't be wasting our money on this stupid event. There is just too much liability."

Chair: "Adam I understand you are not in favor of this idea, but please direct your thoughts towards me and not anyone else. Let's listen to everyone else's thoughts."

Adam: "I doubt that, but whatever."

Chair: "Karen?"

Karen: "Thank you, Chair. Umm…I believe the event is a great idea. We need to make sure we have liability forms for students to sign and we need to make sure we have a proper drainage system near this event to drain the ice once it melts."

Laura and Kim: "Yes, totally. We need liability forms."
Chair: "Adam, Karen has a great idea. If we have liability forms, will you support this?"
Adam: "Yes, I actually might, lets continue our discussion."

That was a basic example of how some of these meetings are run. As a chair you need to be able to step up and intervene when necessary. I have been in meetings where people are yelling at each other across the room and the chair did not do anything. This is your meeting, run it professionally and fairly. Do not tolerate anyone who is disrespectful and make sure to ask for everyone's input on the agenda items.

How to Handle yourself during Meetings

Besides running meetings, you will also be invited to a plethora of meetings. How you hold yourself during meetings will have a large impact on your public image. Something as simple as saying the wrong word could skew a person's impression of you. Dressing the wrong way could also affect people's view of you. In my case, I chose to wear a suit for every meeting throughout my term. Immediately everyone began to view the student government as more professional. All I did was wear a suit, yet it left a tremendous impact on the image of the organization I was representing.

Standing Up When Speaking

This is one of the most important pieces of advice I can give you. As student leaders you will attend numerous meetings where high level administrators are present. For example, I attended monthly meetings for the University President's advisory board which consisted of all the Deans of the colleges (Engineering, Communications, Business etc.) and her entire executive cabinet. Think of a room filled with 20 of the highest administrators for the campus. During that meeting, the President would update everyone on the status of the university and also required me to provide an update. I had given plenty of speeches in front of large groups so speaking was not a problem, but standing up and doing something different than everyone else was a little nerve wracking. Soon enough, it became a habit and I was standing up at every large meeting to speak. It can be a little intimidating in the beginning, but standing up during meetings displays confidence and authority. Any time you speak standing up, you are guaranteed everyone's utmost attention, especially if no one else is standing up. It will also allow you to project your voice clearly allowing everyone to see and hear you better. If you are sitting in a large meeting room, it is easier to be heard standing up than sitting down.

Trust me when I say this, standing up when speaking is rewarding. It will take some time to get used to. In the beginning my legs would shake when I stood up to speak, but I pushed through the shaky leg phase and learned to speak confidently. I recommend this method of speaking when you are in large meetings consisting of more than 15 people.

It is important to recognize that while this can be an effective tool, the way you speak and the context of your speech must be considered. In many instances it is inappropriate to stand while in others it can be the difference between making an impact and being forgotten.

Your Reports

Whenever you are providing an update do not come unprepared to the meeting, especially if it's a meeting with an important official or administrator of the university. Before any meeting, jot down the progress you have made with your projects. This way you can speak

confidently and in an organized fashion. Keep these reports short and to the point.

Acknowledging Others

I came across an administrator who would always publicly thank and acknowledge people for their efforts. I realized how important this was early on during my term. If I felt this great when she spoke, why couldn't I do the same to others? When you speak do so with passion, be genuine, and always acknowledge and thank everyone who has supported you or done something worth recognizing. Give them a shout out, shining the light on other people and their accomplishments is a great way to build moral and positive relationships.

Professionalism

Always come to meetings with a notepad, pen, your business cards, and wearing the proper attire. This shows you are ready to get to work and you mean business.

Speak up

Any meeting you attend; you are representing a group of students. Always speak up for what you believe in. If you are in a meeting where someone shuts down your idea, be persistent and do not give up easily. After all, if you do not stand up for them, who will?

KEY CONCEPTS

1. Meetings can be extremely productive if you have a proper agenda and can run it efficiently.

2. Conducting efficient meetings means the following:

   a. Having an agenda
   b. Keeping minutes
   c. Keeping everything timely
   d. Utilizing Robert's Rules of Order

3. If you are giving a report in a meeting, make sure to prepare your report before hand in an organized manner.

4. Always acknowledge others and give them credit for their work publicly.

5. Dress and act professional during all meetings, no matter how small.

6. Above all, speak up! Any meeting you attend as a student leader is another meeting where you can make a difference.

MY REFLECTION

NICHOLAS AYALA | STUDENT BODY PRESIDENT
SAN JOSE STATE UNIVERSITY

Throughout my time as a San Jose State University Spartan, I was fortunate to be involved in a variety of student organizations. Whether it was Associated Students Government, Delta Sigma Phi Fraternity, Entrepreneurial Society, or Residence Hall Government – having meetings seemed to be the one constant throughout each of them. As an individual who had the opportunity to be involved as well as lead these meetings, there were many key concepts that I will keep in the back of my mind far beyond my collegiate life.

Growing up, we were told to "not judge a book by its cover," but in reality, that is sometimes the only thing we can judge by. When I was President of San Jose State University's Associated Students and SJSU's chapter of Delta Sigma Phi Fraternity, there were multiple occasions where I interacted with University administration, City of San Jose officials, or representatives of the nearby neighborhood associations. As many of these individuals I met with were seasoned professionals, I did not want to give them any doubt in my ability to speak competently about the topics of the meetings. Dressing professionally, speaking clearly and confidently, and researching the topics of discussion in advance are skills that had helped me make the best first impression.

Chairing meetings come with two challenges: running the meeting efficiently and motivating those in attendance. During the first two years of being actively involved in student organizations, I had no idea what Robert's Rule of Order was.

In many cases, because I did not understand the rules, it was harder for me to participate and voice my opinions. In turn, it made it harder for me to really understand the meetings. Learning Robert's Rule of Order was the best investment of my time. Not only did I understand its importance, but it also enabled me to voice my opinions in an efficient manner.

One of the biggest responsibilities of a leader is empowering others around you. Taking the time to really help them understand concepts, such as Robert's Rules of Order, or the "why" of the topics on the agenda makes for a more fruitful meeting for everyone.

11. WORKING IT OUT: COMPROMISE & LEADERSHIP

ROHULLAH LATIF | FORMER STUDENT BODY PRESIDENT
CSUF FULLERTON

What is the point of having a student government? To have individuals representing the large masses whom have similar interests so they can advocate clearly to the administration, right? Many student leaders who have been in the game for a long time develop a mentality of "It's them against the university." Wrong! This mentality will not get you far in your position. I have seen student leaders who were excellent leaders yet could not learn to compromise. They treated others with disrespect and lacked professionalism. Their actions created a lot of distrust between the administration and the student government, which ultimately led to the Student Body President resigning. In order to make changes you have to be willing to communicate and find consensus with the other people who are part of the decision-making. Work with your administration, but do not let them control your decisions. Trust your team of students, and understand that you do not know everything.

The second you begin to think you are always right, is the second you lose appreciation for the people whose experience and expertise exceeds yours as a young professional. The best way to work with people is to first understand who they are and what they stand for. Learn to recognize these leaders and learn how and when to compromise with them.

Student Leaders

Student leadership is not easy. An ineffective student leader could be the downfall of the entire organization. Dealing with a student leader who is not doing a great job can be tough for multiple reasons. Below you will find the different student leaders you might encounter during your term:

Person #1

They have a power trip and they think they know better than you.

Person #2

They are way over their heads and did not expect the position to be this time consuming and difficult.

Person #3

They are in the position for the perks (title, free parking, etc.).

Working with Person # 1

This one is a little difficult because you cannot go into a meeting with this person thinking you know better than them. You cannot challenge them directly on anything in front of other people. Their guard is usually down when they are alone. Schedule a private meeting with them and express how you feel about a certain decision or action. Here is an example of this type of an occurrence:

Dana is the chair of the Student Body Senate and Angela and Danny are senators. During the board meeting Dana keeps cutting off Angela and Danny when they speak. At one point Danny had enough.

Danny: "Dana you are the worst chair we have ever had, quit cutting me off!"

Dana: "Excuse me!? Maybe if you stop talking nonsense and stop wasting everyone's time, I wouldn't have to cut you off!"

Everyone looks at Danny at this point and watches him storm out of the meeting. After the meeting is over Angela asks to meet with Dana.

Angela: "Hey Dana, I understand you are just doing your job as chair, but why did you keep cutting me off. I really had something important I wanted to say, but felt unimportant when I was cut off. I am just trying to do my job as a senator and wanted to express the thoughts of my constituents."

Dana: "Angela, I apologize for doing that. We had a speaker scheduled and I needed to make sure the conversations were kept short, so they had enough time during the meeting. I have been working nonstop to make sure this event goes well and didn't have much help putting the event together."

Angela: "I understand; is there a way I can maybe help you out next time?"

Dana: "Yes, that would be great! Once again, I apologize for cutting you off. Next time I will ask for more help and set a proper schedule so everyone has enough time to express their thoughts."

Pretty simple right? Dana is a leader who easily loses her cool and will blow off on anyone who tells her she is a terrible chair. When Danny confronted her directly in front of everyone, Dana lost it! Angela, on the other hand, had a private meeting with her, disarmed her, and asked to help her. That approach is much more effective than simply confronting someone in front of all their colleagues.

Working with Person #2

During your term, you will definitely encounter at least one if not more leaders like this. They underestimated the difficulty of this position. They probably did not conduct enough research and thought this would be an excellent way to add something on their resume. They did not realize the amount of meetings they would have to attend, the pressure of making all the decisions, or even budgeting the funds. In addition to their leadership role, they need to find time for work, spending time with family and friends and school.

Dealing with this type of person will require you to speak with them privately and ask them if they need any help. Chances are, they do and they will gladly accept any help you can provide. Be understanding of anything they might be going through personally. If all else fails and it seems as if the leader is just not committed any more and will not be able to carry out the requirements set forth in the job description, then it's time to take it a step further. Once again this is if all else fails. Meaning you and many others have tried to help this leader yet the situation is not improving, then it will be time to ask for their resignation. If they do not comply, you can collect evidence against them and take it to the appropriate party who will decide their fate. Sometimes we have leaders that should not be in certain positions. Their presence brings down morale and the organization. No one will volunteer or put any effort for an organization if they do not believe in their leaders.

Working with person #3
They have just lost interest and are in the position for the title, free parking, and other benefits. Some student leadership roles provide many amenities and benefits. My campus comprised of 40,000 students, so you could imagine parking and getting to classes was tough. Luckily, as a student leader I had priority registration and faculty/staff parking. How awesome is that right!? Many schools have different perks in order to motivate students to take on leadership roles. However, while these perks are incentives for student leaders to do their job it can also backfire. These positions may attract people who will only do the bare minimum if they work at all. Dealing with these individuals is similar to dealing with person #2. Since they are incentive driven you could use their

incentive and hold them accountable for their work.

Administration

I was blessed with an awesome administration during my term and had a trusting relationship with everyone in the administration. Yet I knew of colleagues who were not as fortunate as I was. They spent hours arguing and not getting anywhere with administration or even with their own executive directors. Just like student leaders, there are different types of administrators that you will have to learn to identify and work with.

The Awesome Administrator

Here is something that will make you happy. There are more of these types than any other! These administrators love their job and love serving the students. They are not driving their own personal agenda but just want to see students grow as leaders. I have personally come across many of these individuals and have learned a lot from them. Working with them is fairly easy since they will allow you to express your own opinions, ideas, and will only chime in to give you advice based on their experience. Great to have them as an advisor.

The Pleaser Administrator

They will do anything to please the student leader, mainly because they would like something in return. That something is not necessarily bad. It could be they want your support for a vote to build a new building or they need your support to go lobby on behalf of the school.

Remember this type of administrator is not someone you should be wary of; they are harmless, but still be vigilant. Be careful with what they offer you and what you accept. It's all a political game. Things will go south, if you start accepting their gifts in return for any type of support.

The Two-Sided Administrator

Like the student leader who was in over their head, this administrator is tired of working with students and has no patience anymore. They will not entertain any of your ideas, are often quiet at meetings, or controlling. Luckily I have not come across this yet, but I know others who have. The best way to deal with them is to compromise. Take extreme measures if and only if you have tried every other outlet.

There was a student leader who was able to convince the entire student body to support a bill for a vote of no confidence to remove one of the Vice Presidents of the university. That would be something that is considered extreme, but if it is necessary, then do it.

Faculty

Faculty members teach the courses. They also hold a lot of institutional history about the university that could come in handy when making decisions. Much like you have board meetings, so do the faculty. They typically elect a chair and have an executive board similar to your organization. If you are elected president or a representative of the organization, you may appear at this meeting and introduce yourself. During my term, I would have monthly meetings with the chair of that group. Together we planned the first ever student vs faculty basketball game. Great fortunes will come to those who learn to collaborate. If you are not a student body president, it still recommended you attend their meetings once in a while to understand their process.

Staff

Last but certainly not least is the staff. This is everyone that supports the administration, faculty, and student leaders. Think of the staff as the gatekeepers to everyone. If you do not respect or develop a relationship with the gatekeepers, setting up meetings with the right people may become difficult. When I was elected President, I directly oversaw three clerical staff members for my office who would help my team. Treat them with respect and always try to involve them in the process.

Having said that, make sure to draw the line when it comes to sharing too much information. You will be dealing with sensitive information and cannot share the information with everyone. Keep this in mind when you are speaking to your staff. Even if they have been there for 20 years and know everything about the school, they are not your advisors.

When it comes to asking advice for certain decisions do not directly go to your staff, instead seek advice from your advisor or your personal team. Do not vent about other student leaders or administration to your staff either. It could come back to haunt you in the future. Regardless of who you are working with remember, you get more flies with honey than vinegar.

WARNING! This next sentence will break any student leader's heart but it must be said:

"Student leadership is temporary."

It's a good thing because ultimately you will graduate. In reality, the administration could just wait you out. If their ideas do not align with the students, then they could always just wait until they find another student who can get the job done. This is not necessarily a bad thing. Maybe the student leader is not fit for the position, or has a vendetta against the school and simply refuses to cooperate. In that case the administration is simply trying to do their best to work with the students, yet the leaders are not willing to work together. There are always two sides to a story. Leadership could be weak on the student leader's side just as much as on the administration side. Below is an example of the above scenario.

Scenario #1: Against the University

Ever since his first year at school, Joe has been around leaders who were completely against the administration and does not trust them. He eventually became the Student Body President, yet still held on to those beliefs. So when the administration proposed a student fee increase to help open up more classes, Joe was completely against the idea and stormed out of the room. When interviewed by the newspapers, he publicly accused the university of fraud and for trying to take advantage of the students. He did not even allow this to be put on the ballot for students to decide.

Scenario #2: Working with, Not Against
This example is about my university's student fee increase. During one of my meetings with the administrations, a student fee increase was proposed. As any student leader would, I became skeptical. Several thoughts raced through my head.

- Are they trying to take advantage of the students?
- Have they tried this before and maybe it did not work last time, so they are trying to work their magic on me?

I needed time to think before making my decision so I went back to my office to collect my thoughts. Later, I found out that this same student fee process had occurred at a different school, so I called up my colleague for advice. She mentioned how her school's process was completely unfair and the student leaders were taken advantage of. This is when networking can really help you through a tough time. Always network and get to know student leaders at different schools. It really helps to ask advice from a leader who is dealing with the same ordeal. I then scheduled a meeting with my trusted advisors and reviewed the information provided to me. As a leader, it is always beneficial for you to have a group of 4 people who can advise you on your job and a huge emphasis on only advise you!

I realized my university was struggling because California public schools received a drastic cut in the education budget. There were not enough classes being offered, our library was in poor condition, the career center needed funding for programs, and our athletic program was in jeopardy. I also waited until I collected feedback from my constituents regarding their stance. After researching and thinking this thoroughly, I decided to support the fee along the way. Half-way through the process, we decided there were some improvements that needed to be made. Luckily we had excellent administrators who worked with us to make the process more efficient and fair. Overall with the help of student leaders and administrators, we passed the fee in a transparent and fair manner. We later found out, other schools wanted to mimic our process because it yielded agreement from both the students and the administration.

Do you see the difference of how I handled it as opposed to Joe? It's great to stay on your toes and to keep the administration on their toes, but do not lose sight of the real mission. Everyone's mission is to serve the students. Ultimately, the students will end up suffering if one side begins to think their personal mission is more important.

Buy-in

Now let's talk about the concept of "buy-in." I will present you with a scenario. After you read it, take a moment to stop and think of how you would handle this.

Electronic Board Scenario

You just won an election and part of your platform was to install a 5' x 10' electronic message board on one of the school buildings. You are facing some criticism from your peers because they do not think it's possible. The price itself is $110,000, not including the price of painting and cleaning up the building that you want to put it on, which is another $40,000. You also have to convince the university to even entertain the idea of putting something on their building and to chip in the $40,000. So how would you go about working with both students and administration to accomplish this goal? Close the book and take a few minutes to come up with a game plan.

It is tough to come up with a plan that will appease both sides, is it not? That is when the concept of buy-in becomes so important. In the beginning of this project, I conducted a thorough research about the challenge at hand. Luckily, one of our executive directors liked the idea and helped me. He helped me collect different bids, map out the exact location to install the electronic board, completed the budgeting for it, and helped me organize all the data in a complete PowerPoint. Then I presented this information and had to convince my board and the rest of the student leaders. The best way to convince anyone of an idea is to make your idea their idea. I made sure to have mandatory meetings with the two student leaders who would be key players. I collected their ideas and asked for their advice regarding the entire project. I even put them in charge of some details. If they had questions or concerns, then I would have the answers. The goal is to have their voices be heard and make them apart of the decision making process. People will run with an idea if and only if they have some say in the overall process and have a role to play in accomplishing the goal at hand. When I gave reports at public meetings regarding the project, I would give them credit and continuously thank them for helping me. If anything went wrong, I would immediately take full responsibility without the mention of anyone else's name. After all, great leaders give credit and take the blame.

Once I had the support of my organization, I scheduled meetings with the University President, the Vice President of Finance for the university, the University Police, the Athletics Department, and the people in charge of the facilities.

During the meetings, I listed all the benefits of having this electronic board. It would increase the communication between the university and the students, thus increasing student involvement and pride. I mentioned how this will also benefit the university's athletic department because they would be able to advertise all their games to students on the other side of the campus. Not to mention, the university police could also use the electronic board for emergency purposes. I had all the key players in the room and I made all of stakeholders.

In the end, the university and student body both agreed to become partners and pay their respective shares. Sounds easy, right? It really is, if you can learn to work with people. You just need to listen to their concerns and get them to "buy-in" to your idea.

Key Players in your University

You cannot just come to a meeting and expect anyone to buy-in to your idea if you have not established a relationship with that person. Before my term started, I made sure to meet and have lunch or coffee with all the campus leaders and established a relationship with them. It's the idea of "social capital." It's not about bartering, it's about being willing to give and get what you expect from others. Treating people with respect, fulfilling your promises, and being willing to help others accomplish their goals, should be a priority for you. Before my term started, I made an effort to meet the following people on my campus:

University President

Your life will be a lot easier, if you can learn to work together. You do not need to be best friends, but make sure you establish mutual respect for each other. That means, do not badmouth your president in front of the media. Anything you say against the President of the

University will partially reflect your character as well. Be good to your president and they will be good to you. If they are not doing their job, then and only then can you resort to different methods.

Director of Parking

Parking is terrible on most campuses and parking permits are expensive. If any parking issues (parking fee's increase) come up during your term, you will have already met the person in charge.

University Police

It is always nice to know your university Chief of Police. I invited my Chief of Police over to the student body office and gave him a tour of our building. Afterwards, he became one of my trusted and respected advisors.

Athletic Director

You cannot have school pride without the help of your athletic director. With his help we were able to put on pep rallies and increase student attendance at games. Our relationship was so strong, that the athletic department even raffled off an entire Hawaii trip during one of our joint events. He was one of the best athletic directors I had ever worked with because he was selfless and was open to working with students.

Academic Senate Chair

This person is in charge of the main meeting for the entire faculty. Together, we would brainstorm different ideas on how to approach different issues at hand and we even had a joint event (Student vs. Faculty Basketball game) that has become tradition now.

The Deans of each College

Each major has their own respective dean who manages that college. It is important for you to meet these leaders so you can efficiently conduct outreach programs to specific colleges and majors.

The Council that Oversees All of Your Clubs and Organizations

Some campuses have student groups that oversee clubs and organizations. Developing a relationship with them is a great way to communicate your efforts to a student body that is already engaged.

There is a bigger problem than just two parties not getting along. Guess who will suffer if the relationship between the administrators and the students is not good? The students will suffer, the same students whom you represent and took an oath to serve. So please put aside any issues you have or might have with the administration. Work with them so they can work with you. Only and only when you learn to work together can you truly fulfill your role as a student leader. Will you put aside your differences for the betterment of your campus?

KEY CONCEPTS

1. A collegiate university offers a very diverse atmosphere for student leaders to sharpen their communication skills.

2. As a student leader you need to be able to work with 4 different types of campus leaders: Student leaders, Administrators, Faculty and Staff.

3. Communicating with a student leader is different than communicating with an administrator, staff person, or faculty member.

4. The best way to get buy-in from any type of leader is to make your idea their idea.

5. Before you start your term, schedule a meeting with all the key players in your university.

MY REFLECTION

HARPREET BATH | STUDENT BODY PRESIDENT
CALIFORNIA STATE UNIVERSITY, FULLERTON

When I was running for student body president, I thought I knew what issues students cared about and that I would, upon getting elected, advocate on behalf of them and get those necessary changes through. As I started working on the issues and ideas, I realized that in order to get anything done at a university, you need to be able to work with people and bring them onboard to be successful and none of that is possible without compromise.

I first learned about this at the beginning of my term when I wanted to change the number of students on the student fee committee which oversaw all campus fees and recommended changes to the president. The initial proposal that I submitted was 9 students and 6 administrators/faculty/staff. That proposal was quickly refuted by a proposal of 7 students and 6 faculty and staff. Upon numerous discussions with the administration, we were able to come to a consensus of 8 students and 6 administrators/faculty/staff and the student body president was to become co-chair of the committee alongside the VP of Student Affairs.

This was especially important because no other university in our system had more than a 1 student majority on the student fee committee and now my campus had a 2 student majority along with a co-chair title. That compromise between the administration and I opened up new levels of trust and venues to create similar large-scale changes on our campus.

Compromise is not about being politically savvy or pulling favors or forcing people to your demands. Compromise is recognizing what is fair and working hard to help others recognize that and then finding a middle ground to achieve it.

12. COMMUNICATION & PUBLIC SPEAKING

TAYLOR HERREN | PRESIDENT
CALIFORNIA STATE STUDENT ASSOCIATION

Communication is the channel to create and maintain relationships and the vehicle that carries information. Communicating successfully is the key to earning the trust of your constituents and creating buy-in from the stakeholders you need to collaborate with in order to create change. As a student leader, the idea of mastering several types of communication methods is particularly important. You are elected to be the voice of the students. The only way to fulfill that fiduciary responsibility is by having constant and widespread communication with all the people who are connected and touched by the work you perform. When communicating with people or groups, make sure you keep the following in mind:

- Know your audience
- Understand the rules of engagement
- Create a system that works for you
- Listen more than you speak
- Remember that you are always communicating

Know Your Audience
It does not matter what the group size, setting, or time is. It does not matter if you are in a personal meeting or a large event. What matters much more is that you know

your audience. As a liaison you must be comfortable interacting with students, faculty, staff, administration, city officials, community members, and even elected representatives.

We often hear about the importance of confidence when it comes to successful communicators, in particular when it comes to public speaking. As important as it is to be articulate, I believe it is even more crucial to be able to connect with and speak in a manner your audience can understand and relate to. Being prepared prior is the key to successfully accomplishing this aspect of effective communication. Make an effort to research and understand the demographics and backgrounds of your audience. Is there a specific reason they are attending the engagement where you are speaking? Is there is specific organization hosting? If so, what are their mission and values? This information is valuable for public speeches, oral reporting, and answering questions at general meetings.

If you are meeting with an individual, prepare an agenda in advance with an understanding of their affiliations, responsibilities and/or current areas of interest. Start your conversation with a question or a statement about the focus of their work. Tailoring your message and delivery in a way that is relatable and appropriate will help you be successful in sharing your message with any group or stakeholder. Understand the reason or purpose of that particular engagement. Are you going to promote or ask for something or are you attending because you were asked? What you are saying should align with the reason you are in attendance. There should always be a point or a take-away for listeners and it should be determined before you say anything.

As Student Body President, I had a countless number of meetings, events, and programs I would be asked to either attend or speak at. During the summer I would attend the orientations for incoming students and share the student experience at Chico State. At the same time, I also attended the Academic Senate, where I would also describe the student experience. At orientation, I discussed things like residential life, on campus events, and study abroad programs. In the presence of faculty, I focused on topics like class sizes/availability, undergraduate research opportunities, and internship programs. At the orientation, my purpose was to introduce my peers to the most popular services and programs with the intention of connecting them to those opportunities at the start of college. In the Academic Senate, I brought up the things that impacted teaching and learning with the goal of improving the classroom experience for students. I appreciated that an audience of incoming students is drastically different from one that is made up of university faculty. I focused on what I felt was most pertinent to each group and their respective interests. Use this tactic to your advantage. Whether you are running for election or going to different clubs and organizations to give a presentation, relay information that is pertinent to the specific audience. If it does not affect them in any shape or form, leave it out of your message altogether.

Generally speaking, you can classify the scenarios that will require you to practice communication skills into three categories; personal interactions, meetings, and public speaking engagements and presentations. By creating personal relationships and being genuine with people in a one-on-one setting, you will create and execute a vision that includes both your own personal initiatives and the issues that are most important to students.

Rules of Engagement
Create personal relationships that are genuine. Do this by getting to know people and develop personal relationships with the people you meet. It will allow you to create and execute a vision that includes both your own personal initiatives and the issues that are most important to students. It may be simple advice, but talk, react, and respond to others in a way that you would want to be treated.

When you are reporting on behalf of students, share the concerns that students have shared with you. If a student comes to you with an idea, your job is to find the right people who can give you the answers to make those ideas a reality. As a representative, being a liaison is your duty and you have a responsibility to take the student voice into as many decision making discussions as possible. You have access to many of the people who have the information that will determine your success with campus-wide projects.

Take full advantage of the seat you have at the table as a student representative. Always prepare an agenda prior to attending any meeting. Even if there is an agenda prepared, always have talking points and a list of things you need to accomplish. This could be a concern or issue that needs to be addressed or a question that needs an answer. Going in prepared gives you the ability to direct the conversation as a participant.

When it comes to anything that is a presentation or formal speaking engagement you should spend a significant amount of time planning and preparing beforehand. There are two simple steps to prepare for opportunities like this. First, write the speech out completely to ensure your comments are organized, succinct and, within the time allocated. Practice until you can confidently recite that speech without notes. Being free of notes will allow you to connect with the audience by using body language to read and interact with your audience.

There are two types of communications you should expect to engage in regularly. The first being personal communication and the second in a large group setting. When you are reporting on behalf of students, make the most of the opportunities you have to either submit a written report or give a verbal one. Share the current initiatives of students and report on the current issues that are affecting the student body.

When engaging in decision-making conversations that impact students, take full advantage of the seat you have at the table as a student representative. Always prepare an agenda prior to attending any meeting. Even if there is an agenda prepared, ensure to always have talking points and a list of things you need to accomplish. This could be a concern or issue that needs to be addressed or a question that needs an answer. Going in prepared gives you the ability to direct the conversation as a participant.

Create a System that Works for You

Creating a system that allows you to diligently check and respond to emails is not only a key to success, but is a foundational skill you must master in order to stay connected with those you are accountable to. You need to be prepared to read and respond to any and every email that comes to you. There are many accepted ways to write an email. People will use all types of introductions, salutations, formats, etc. Do not worry about perfectly conforming to anything. It is much more important that your email is titled and addressed correctly and that you diligently proofread it to make sure it is edited and accurate. Learning how to be concise yet remain professional when writing an email will allow you to build relationships through this venue while keeping you connected to an extensive network of people. Your time will only become more valuable as the year progresses, so the faster you get through emails, the better. Speedy responses tend to impress those you are communicating with while allowing you to maintain control of your inbox.

When I first started in my position, I used to write these beautifully detailed emails. I remember writing my first email to my university president and spent 30 minutes to complete. At the time, I was proud that I had spent so much time putting it together. In hindsight, the president probably spent less than a minute reading that email. On the other hand, being diligent about checking and responding to email is equally important. Responding to emails in a timely manner will get people the information and answers they need from you. You also do not want to send emails that are filled with mistakes because it will impact your credibility. It will be up to you to find that balance.

Listen More

Many of us have become leaders because of our confidence in our voice. As important as it is to speak up for your constituents, it is equally vital you listen to what they have to say. This will allow you to make the right decisions when you are speaking for them. Even more so, it will allow you to understand the diverse experiences and opinions of the student population you represent. It is essential that you are proactive in your listening so that you can absorb and understand as much information as possible. What you are expected to be familiar with is vast and the only way to keep up is to be attentive and productive in any all meetings. You should know what is on the agenda and how it impacts students before you walk into the meeting room. You have an obligation to keep your constituents informed. You are more than the collective voice of the students; you are also their eyes and ears. Pay very close attention when you are attending meetings as the student representative and, more importantly, find a way to get that information back to students.

Be genuine and aim to "share" instead of "speak" with the idea that "sharing" should include things that are relevant and come from a genuine place. Any person could technically speak to people. True leaders can authentically share in a way that connects to those listening. The importance of using inclusive and empowering language cannot be overstated. Using inclusive language means that you are considerate of the way you say things as it relates to how it makes people feel. This is as simple as speaking in a calm tone so that people feel you are being respectful. It can be more complicated when you are talking about specific "trigger words." For example, you do not want to walk into a room and address the group with a "hey guys." "Guys" is a term used to describe men and if there are any women in the room you are excluding them in your introduction by using that term. Using empowering language is equally important. Speaking in a way that includes other people's ideas and words like "we", "us", and "ours" makes people feel like they are a part of the things you are discussing. People like to listen to someone they can relate to and engage in a venue where they feel respected and connected to what is being said.

You Are Always Communicating

I am sure you have heard the saying "body language is the most important form of communication." People will pay as much attention to how you carry yourself in public as they do to what you say. It is also true that your body language has an impact on the way people perceive your message. When you are not physically invested in being somewhere or with someone your mind is not either.

Holding yourself with confidence and respect can help both you and the people you are communicating with remain invested. When it comes to university meetings, you are often the only student in the room and need to have a posture that shows you are attentive and engaged in whatever is going on. Even if you are walking on campus, make sure to smile and greet everyone with a warm and genuine smile. Have confidence in your own style of speaking and interacting with others. Learn to be comfortable as yourself. Being well-rounded in your communication skills is the key to being successful in every situation in which you find yourself.

Your ability to communicate with all types of people in a wide variety of ways will determine the degree to which projects are brought to fruition and which tasks are accomplished. Good communication is a two-way street. One side is about gathering information from all the stakeholders so that you can be informed and educated about your campus community. The other allows you to inform the decision-makers on your campus about what students are experiencing and want to see happen. Learn and work to further the skills needed to drive on both sides of this street by connecting with people through respectful, professional, and concise communication.

KEY CONCEPTS

1. Prepare your style and content based on who you will be communicating with and the purpose of the event.

2. Everything from writing professional emails to interacting with people in between classes, always remember to maintain a professional front.

3. Have a very good understanding of your audience in terms of their beliefs and interests. You should always describe the purpose for your speech and what your overall outcome is for communicating with that person or group.

4. Listen more, talk less. People want to be heard, and want you to value their ideas and point of view.

5. Be confident, as both a verbal and nonverbal communicator.

6. Be genuine by "sharing" instead of "speaking." Using inclusive and empowering language allows you to include other people. Recognize the audience, their identity, and values that are important to them.

7. The key to successful communication is preparation.

MY REFLECTION

KEYRA GALVANCO | CHAIR OF THE YOUTH EMPOWERMENT PROGRAM
SANTA CLARA UNIVERSITY

Public Speaking has not always been my strength. You look at me now and say, "how can that possibly be?" It took me a few years to realize that my fear for large crowds was not the problem. I struggled early on with an insecurity I carried for a long time and that was self-identification. I became part of a non-profit organization for first-generation college students, the Silicon Valley Summer Search Program, where I was forced to step out of my comfort zone. I learned to accept my childhood struggles and not be afraid of outside judgment.

The instant I decided to step out of the parameters of my familial circumstances was the moment I began to witness the changes in my personal and professional development. Joining the Youth Empowerment Program (YEP) at Santa Clara University was the beginning of my role as a student leader on campus. I gave tours to underprivileged middle school and high schools across the bay area and participated in student panels. Public speaking in front of parents, staff members, and students was not the challenge. The challenge was the fear of not being able to relate to my audience. I started living when I chose to rise above the confines of my individualist concerns like fearing what others would think of me and learned to embrace my differences. It was the first time in my life where I was not afraid to step out of my comfort zone and expose myself to that extent. I learned then and there that successful communication with a group of people does not mean talking at them but finding a commonality where both parties can relate and share with them instead. Student panels are the most nerve wracking, especially when confronted with a crowd of high school students. I was never prepared for what they would ask, but one thing was for sure. I did my very best to be as honest as possible because I knew that I lived in their shoes once.

Public speaking, in whatever form, can be something that you can prepare for, but sometimes that is not always the case. In many cases, I found inspiration to speak from the heart in order to get my point across. I believe the biggest gift your audience can takeaway is the ability to relate with a shared experience. Whether you are having a one-on-one conversation or speaking in front of a large crowd in a college campus, using inclusive language to gain a mutual understanding is the best way to keep an audience engaged. With that said, I invite student leaders from all college campuses to look at public speaking as a form of an opportunity to find inclusion among you and your audience. Public speaking certainly takes a lot of practice, but it can definitely be to your advantage to have an audience connect with you right off the bat. There were many times I felt empowered by what someone said and you will be surprised that is often the case.

13. WORKING WITH THE MEDIA

DANIEL CLARK | FORMER PRESIDENT
CALIFORNIA STATE STUDENT ASSOCIATION

Working with the media is absolutely critical to ensuring your message gets out to those who you want to hear it. Media plays a huge role in shaping public discussion and it can also provide a platform for you to showcase what your student government organization is doing. More so, it can build a bridge between your student body and student government. Using the media to cover your events or stories can be a great way to educate your community and students, get support for initiatives you are working on, and raise awareness of a particular issue. Getting the spotlight on you and your organization should not be the main goal, building connections and having access to the media has more benefits than that. Think about media coverage and your relationship with the media as one more tool in your tool-kit.

Newspapers

Before Twitter, social media, and the internet, the only way to get breaking news was to wait 24 hours and get it from the newspaper. Newspapers eventually did get on social media and began to have news online. So why is the newspaper so important? Because of the audience reading the newspaper. Students are not the only ones reading the local paper; community leaders, elected officials, businessmen and businesswomen (potential donors), and other local decision makers are reading as well. The newspaper is broken down into two formats: Daily Newspapers and Weekly Newspapers. Daily newspapers are broken down into different sections including but not limited to, national, local, editorials, opinion editorials, letters to the editors, and feature articles.

Weekly newspapers run in a similar format, but usually are in smaller metropolitan locations. In addition to local media outlets, your campus may have its own newspaper where they have a direct connection with your constituents. In order for your story to reach the newspaper (or any forms of media), it has to come in the form of a press release and understanding how to pitch your story.

Press Releases

A press release is a direct communication link to relay information or a story to any number of media outlets and established organization. If properly written, a press release can be sent to numerous media sources and can be published in a variety of facets. Press releases are a quick and cost effective way to gain exposure of your story or event. The problem with press releases is that so many are poorly written and fail to convey the message that you are trying to articulate. Doing so puts you in danger of looking unprofessional and as someone who the media will not trust. In the media world, words can spread like wildfire. When you are drafting a press release, it's important to break it down into the "who, what, where, when, why, and how" for the journalist. Who is in this story you are pitching and who does it affect? What is happening in the story and where does the story take place (national, local, and campus). When does the story take place (past or future) and why is it newsworthy? How does this story affect the campus and the community?

Two Page Press Release

Your press release should be written as you want it to appear on the front-page. Write what you want the newspaper to say and make sure it is direct and to the point. Your press release should be one page.
If it is longer than one page, then you run the risk of your story not getting printed or even read by very busy journalists. Now that you have a basic understanding of what a press release is, let's take a look at how to properly write one, since doing so can help bring proper media coverage to your events.

Write in Inverted Pyramid Format

Inverted Pyramid Format defined as "a metaphor used by journalists and other writers to illustrate how information should be prioritized and structured in journalistic text." Pyramid format writing looks like this:

Headline

Sub headline

Main idea (who, what, when where, why, and how)

Supporting info/Crucial Info
General Info/ Background Info

Student Leader Book Helps Revolutionize Advocacy
Did that grab your attention? Good. That is the point of
writing your headline. Your headline should be attention-
grabbing, brief, to the point, and clear to understand. It
should be the smaller version of your press releases main
idea. Your headline should be the attention grabber. It
needs to make people want to read your article. Grab the
main idea from your press release and put it into your
headline. If you are having difficulty with the headline,
then do it at the end. By doing the headline at the end,
you can ensure that you got all the work out of the way
and can include the main topics at the top.

Sub Heading Should Add Not Subtract
Right underneath your headline will be the sub heading.
This is where you can have additional information about
your story without making the headline overly long.
When journalists are looking through the plethora of
press releases they receive, the headline and sub-headline
can be the difference of your story getting picked or not.

Body Paragraph
Reporters are busy people (extra emphasis on busy). They
are on tight deadlines and schedules that would make a
college student's class schedule blush. So do the reporter
(and yourself) a favor and make sure everything you're
trying to get out is in the body copy. Your first paragraph

should include your main idea and the paragraphs that follow should be in the inverted pyramid format above. The world is fast paced and information is coming and going quickly, no one has time to go through your press release and search for your main idea.

Just the Main Facts

We have been conditioned in the classroom to provide a thorough analysis of everything. While this is great for academia, this is absolutely terrible for media. Important facts need to put in your press release and if these facts relate to your event or cause then you have added legitimacy to your event. Let the writer be the one to provide the ebb and flow of your main idea. Do not use jargon, repetition, or overly long sentences. Those should be saved for literary analysis work in the classroom, not press releases in the real world.

Mind your Grammar

No matter how great your cause or event is, it will not matter if the journalist uses your press release as an example of what not to do in a journalism class. Nothing kills your cause more than the lack of legitimacy and nothing seems more illegitimate and a waste of more time than a poorly written press release.

A Link to the Past

So you got the journalist attention, now what? Give them more links in case they are interested in doing their own research or wanting to confirm the validity of your information. If the website or link is a third party, as in someone not associated with you, then you make the case even easier for your story to go to print. If you can, provide a supplemental packet to go along with the press release. So long as the press release is short and to the point, then the extra information will help the journalist.

Contact Information is clear and visible

Nothing is more embarrassing than writing a killer press release without any contact information. Ensure that your contact information is clear and visible enough so that you can be reached. Having it in the header or the very end of your press release is appropriate. Make sure to include your email, phone number, name, title or position, and group you're affiliated with. If you include your personal information, it may be put out there in the world. If this is sensitive information, consider using a Google phone number or a separate email.

Pitching the Perfect Story

Now that you have the perfect press release, send your press release to the appropriate news agency. Part of the process involves "pitching" your story. Pitching your story is a great way to convince a journalist or a news broadcaster that your story is not only worth their time, but also relevant to their target market. Ultimately, your pitch should be like a headline, it needs to hook someone in and maintain their attention. While some PR professionals feel that pitching your story is all you need, that is not the case. You are a student and unfortunately, in the minds of many the status of a student is neither that high nor important. Some of you may not have the backing of a huge corporation or non-profit to go hand in hand with your story. So it is important to be persistent, clear, and concise with your message, because you might only have one shot at it.

Author your press release to supplement your pitch to the media. By doing so, you can target specific reporters and news stations. When you are contacting the media ensure that you have the correct facts. Some journalists may follow up with questions when you are making your pitch, so be able to provide answers quickly.

Have a relaxed conversation, but also try to emphasize the importance of the event. Everything you say or write is newsworthy and can be used for or against you. Consider everything "on the record" unless they state otherwise (even then it's better to be safe than sorry). Parts of what you say, even if you did not intend for them to be used, can be printed.

Letters to the Editors

Now that you have learned the basics of press releases and pitching your story, it is time to add more piece to your ever evolving toolbox. Let's say your press release has not gained the attention you expected. What do you do? Write a Letter to the Editor! Letters to editors have been around for years and offer opportunities for community members to give their opinion on the news in the surrounding area. Doing so can help influence public opinion and can potentially compel people to take action, or at the very least provide them information about a topic they may know nothing about. When you are conducting business that revolves around the campus, letters to the editor of your campus newspaper are one way to ensure that your work is being broadcast to your students. By being strategic your letters can help ensure that a particular issue remains in the public spotlight. Letters to the editor offer a chance for your voice to be heard.

Newspapers only have so much print space and if you live in larger metropolitan cities then you are under competition with a variety of folks. A newspaper like the LA Times or New York Times may receive hundreds, if not thousands of letters a day. On the other hand, smaller papers may only receive a few and are more than likely to print what they receive. You will have a higher likelihood of success getting your news to your campus newspaper. Choose your media outlet wisely. Like your press release, the letter to the editor needs to stand out.

Tips for Your Letter to The Editor
- Author your Letter to Editor using the Inverted pyramid format. Just without the bold eye catching headline.
- Use something simple for the salutation like "to the Editor of (Campus Newspaper Name Here)" or "dear, LA Times."

- Your main idea should come first and then everything that follows should supplement your main idea. Explain your main idea in simple terms.

- Keep it brief. Try if possible to keep it under 450 words. Editors will usually cut letters if they are too long, so keep your main ideas at the top.

- Keep it factual. Nothing kills credibility more than something that sounds like it belongs in the National Enquirer. If you are trying to criticize policy or decisions on your campus, try to back it up with other solutions. Remember the community you are living in and the students you serve.

- Feel free to appeal to people's emotions. Unlike press releases, letters to the editors can be a little more informal.

- Send it via email if possible. While actual typed letters are acceptable, emailing it makes it easier for journalists to include it in the paper without retyping or scanning. The original file format is preferred when sending it so that editors can easily edit if needed.

- Sign your letter and include your title or position if possible. Doing so adds authority to your letter and can help increase your chances of getting published. The newspaper will rarely publish 'anonymous" letters. Newspapers usually like to ensure that you actually wrote the letter and will follow up so make sure you include your contact info (you can make a note on the letter that contact info is for the editor's eyes only).

- Newspapers will rarely publish letters that attack or are slanderous in nature. They want to avoid anything being printed that contain false information.
- Your letter did not get published? No problem! Just rewrite your letter using a different angle and send it again at a later time, but make sure your main ideas remain the same.
- Is your letter to the editor extraordinarily long? Then consider writing an opinion editorial or a guest column. Communicate this with the editor ahead of time and it may be wise to have it handy in the event they want to publish ASAP.

Television

Television coverage is more than just sharing a story; it offers an opportunity to visually see coverage first hand. Choosing the audience you want to communicate your story to is important before identifying potential television stations to contact. National news outlets (NBC, CBS, ABC, Fox) and cable news outlets (MSNBC, CNN, FOX News) will likely focus on national stories and events.

Unless your story is of huge historical importance that could likely alter society for millennia, it is best to reach out to your local network affiliate. These local stations cover local stories and are a good way of getting attention for an issue you are advocating or a local event you are hosting. This makes the most sense and can provide you more coverage from the people who are going to care the most: the local community.

Television Interview

Now that you have television coverage it is time to speak to the reporters. What do you do when the cameras are rolling and the lights are flashing?

The key is to relax. Do not sweat it if you mess up. In fact, try not to sweat (it looks bad on camera). The number one thing you could do that would make things difficult for you would be to overreact or get nervous. It is OK to think of the interview as a casual conversation between you and the reporter (which in reality if you take away the camera that is precisely what it is). During the interview, make sure you look the part. It does not matter if you are the president or a board member; you are representing your organization. It is important that you act and look professional throughout the interview. Refrain from using improper language and make sure you are smiling and not fidgeting, as your body language becomes magnified on camera.

Create 3 talking points that cover the main idea of your message. What are the biggest and most important ideas to take away from your interview? Whatever those are, stick to them when you are getting interviewed.
Do not ramble because more than likely you're four-minute interview will be chopped up into sound bites and the reporter will be the one to control what is being broadcasted.

Speak with confidence and authority. You are the EXPERT in what you are talking about: so act accordingly. Head up, eyes forward, and speak with conviction. If the reporter asks a question that you do not have the answer to then be honest. There is nothing wrong with saying "that is a good question, but I do not have that specific information on me right now. Perhaps we can trade business cards and I can get back to you?" or "that is an evolving situation and once we have more information we will release it at a later time." There is nothing worse than lying to a reporter. Not only does that ruin your relationship, but it also ruins the relationship of the organization with that station.

Radio
Radio coverage, like all forms of media, has expanded over recent years. Radio can help share a message with a specific target audience that may not be listening to your message through traditional means. Talk radio and news radio are great ways to ensure that your message is discussed in depth. Unlike print and television, radio can also be a chance for callers to call in and ask questions about particular topics or give you feedback regarding something you are trying to accomplish. Reaching out to morning DJ's can be a great way to get to listeners on their way to school or work. When we were planning a big event at Fresno City College we got in contact with our local radio station who helped bring students to the event. The extra participation was great and the event was bigger than we expected.

Social Media

An evolving communication medium that has formed over recent years is social media. Social media has rapidly changed communication as it has allowed us to share, create, and exchange information at a rapid rate. Social media has put the power in our hands, but with great power comes… well you know the rest. There are many different forms of social media such as microblogs, blogs, social networks, podcasts, online videos, community forums, wikis, and vlogs (to name a few). Entire books have been dedicated to social media, but for simplicity's sake we will be discussing the most used forms of social media. This list consists of Facebook, Twitter, Instagram, Google+, Snapchat, and blogs.

Social Media is here to stay and as such it is important for you to understand the ins and outs or the dos and do nots of social media. As a student leader, you are a publicly elected official and as such it is important to monitor what you put online. Building your image is important not only for you, but for the brand of your organization. Often times your organization will be judged based upon what you are writing (or not writing). Professionalism and etiquette is of the utmost importance when managing your social media accounts. This is not to say that you must censor every single post, unfiltered content may not always be the wisest course of action. Below are a few tips to create a professional presence online.

Positioning yourself Online

How do you want to be seen online? Your image and brand is important to how your constituents view you. Perception is reality. This is the first step to understanding how you want people to view you and what kind of content you want to deliver. You can be seen as someone who starts conversations, someone who provides information for students, or a combination of the two. Most importantly, be personable! Feel free to share some of your stories, especially if it relates to current events on campus.

What Goes on the Internet Stays on the Internet

Be cautious of what you put on social media because it can stay there forever. Tweets and Facebook posts from years ago can be used against you when you're campaigning or just in general. People make mistakes in their youth, but some simple cleanup of your social media can save you a lot of trouble. Before I decided to run for election, I sorted through 1000's of pictures on my Facebook and removed anything that could be perceived negatively. Consider social media to be like working with the newspaper, everything is on record. Students and the media can use what you say on the internet as a quote or use it against you when you are trying to advocate for a certain cause. It would look hypocritical if your goal for the campus is to prevent students' drinking and then you have photos of you binge drinking at bars. Below are some tips to help you navigate through your social media outlets:

- Unless you run a blog that has your daily thoughts and have developed a following, do not air out your dirty laundry online. Consider utilizing an actual diary to vent your frustrations or speak to a friend or school counselor who can help you work things out.
- Nothing kills your credibility more than words that are misspelled or are incorrectly used.
- #Every #Post #Shouldn't #Have #A #Hashtag #That #Looks #Kinda #Weird. Unnecessary hashtags are pointless, it adds clutter to your posts and distracts from the post. They can take away from or interfere with the message. The purpose of a hashtag is to tag posts with certain words so they can be viewed together. Using them in your microblog or social media platform can be a fantastic way to get the message out to your students.

Friends & Following Everyone

While your social media is your platform to share information with your constituents, you do not need to add every single person who sends you a friend request or requests to follow you. Your social media is your social media. Do not feel pressured to add strangers if it makes you feel uncomfortable. Your safety will always be a priority. Student first, leader second. In any case, you can always create another account for your leadership activities.

Solve Problems

If a constituent brings an issue to your attention, make sure to remedy the problem openly and honestly. The worst thing you can do with social media is to get defensive when issues come to light or to ignore them. If you do not have the answer to something and cannot get the answer in a timely manner, there is nothing wrong with answering "that is a very good question, I do not have the answer but I will be sure to follow up with you soon. Please email me at (insert email) so that I may respond appropriately."

Being open and transparent is important in dealing with criticism or issues. I have seen student leaders get scrutinized for arguing with students online. Avoid any and all debates and arguments online.

KEY CONCEPTS

1. Working with the media is absolutely critical to ensuring your message gets out to those who you want to reach.

2. Every media platform has its pros and cons. Know them before trying to articulate your message.

3. Newspapers are great for reaching a wide array of people at a minimum of cost for you or the organization.

4. A press release is the communication link between the media outlet and your story.

5. Television networks have one of the largest audiences. If you have an opportunity to get on air, do so strategically and carefully.

6. Social media is evolving, evolve with it. Social media is not your diary. Do not air out dirty laundry.

MY REFLECTION

LOURDES AMENTE | FORMER STUDENT BODY PRESIDENT
SAN JOSE STATE UNIVERSITY

In any story there's usually a beginning, middle and an end. In the story there is typically a hero, a villain, a conflict and resolution. Most storybooks will begin with, "once upon a time…" but in news, "If it bleeds, it leads," is what I was taught in when it came to news reporting. Sitting in a public relations class at a community college when I was in high school sparked my interest to be in media. I would watch the news and I would see this light mocha colored Filipino-American woman report in the 6:30am news. Watching her made motivated and gave me hope.

When I was a graduating senior in high school, I was provided the opportunity to be part of a four-year paid internship program where I would be partnered with one of the top leading media companies in the world. Within the city of Los Angeles, California, my dreams and aspirations of working in media were almost the same as the other thousands wanting the same opportunity.

In my experience, I was able work in two major crucial sectors of media; corporate diversity and entertainment diversity. I got to experience the behind the scenes meetings and decision-making processes related to diversity in media. Now yes everyone can vent their opinions away and say that media is still lacking diversity, I on the other hand am a product of how this company provided me, a multiethnic, first-generation, woman, the opportunity in media.

Companies want to see dedication and commitment to your own moral values. They want to see diverse talent and provide them with the opportunities to flourish in the industry. Every time the underdog is seen in a minor role, they advocate and root for them to be in the major roles. Sometimes the underdog wins, and sometimes they lose. When they do lose, they learn to persevere and try again. In student government, I advocated for not only for the underrepresented individuals but also for all 32,500+ students at San Jose State University. No matter what background ethnicity, gender, sexual orientation, age, or ability one may have, I wanted to provide these talented and unique individuals with the opportunities to excel higher education. As the previous President & CEO, of Associated Students at San Jose State University my personal core value is to enhance and advocate for student success in higher education and in my institution.

From my experience of working in corporate and entertainment diversity, it has provided me the early on experience to develop my knowledge of diversity and inclusion and translate that knowledge into my higher educational experience. The best part of my experience is that I get to develop my own mini-chapters to the story of my life. Although, my story may be different from yours, the various stories make-up the diverse body in a company and a university.

14. STAY GROUNDED
TAYLOR HERREN | PRESIDENT
CALIFORNIA STATE STUDENT ASSOCIATION

Being a student leader does not end with election day results; quite the contrary, that's when it all starts. With your title comes a slew of emotions - excitement, doubt, eagerness, fear, and hope. At the end of the day, no matter how you feel, you have to remember one thing: you are not your emotions. And this applies to all your days in office, the highest of the highs and the lowest of the lows. What is important is that you stay grounded. But what does this mean for a student leader in the day to day grind of balancing student leadership and your personal life and values?

Being a Student

It can be easy to forget you are in school for one main reason: to graduate with a degree. If you are anything like me in the office, you could easily find yourself "working" away for hours without ever even thinking of doing homework. Work may not be working for you. Student advocacy may not be a position for you; it can be a passion that comes so naturally, that it flows from you. At the heart of it all, however, is one thing: you are a student first. You have a responsibility not only to your constituents, but also to yourself, to carry out your academic career with as much commitment and vigor as you are putting into your leadership position. This is not to say you cannot hold your studies and your office at the same level of priority. Bring your "A" game in the classroom and to your meetings. The most successful individuals in life are not great in one area and so-so in another; they gain mastery on every level of their life. That mastery starts here. Your role as a student leader goes beyond your years in school or time in the office. This position could be a defining moment in your life but do not let it prevent you from graduating and pursuing other endeavors in your life that could potentially open more doors.

Self-care

Schedule meetings with your academic counselors, finding and utilizing mentors, participating in study groups, plan your week ahead of time (including events, socials, and personal responsibilities), set and actually write down your academic and professional goals, and above all else, make sure to take care of yourself. Self-care can be one of the most difficult things to keep mindful of while in office. It is not easy balancing school, extracurricular activities, work, and personal responsibilities. Taking on the role of student leader should not be seen as a burden or just "another thing I have to do." If it's truly something you are doing because you genuinely believe in what you are working toward, then it is something you get to do. This can be difficult to keep in mind, however, when you find yourself sleep deprived, starving (because you simply forgot to eat), and depleted of energy. Maintaining a healthy diet, getting a good night's rest, and getting normal amounts of exercise, can easily improve your health. We all know eating, and sleeping are all important factors to living a healthy lifestyle; but just because we know it does not mean we practice it. Below are a few ways to keep all three in mind:

Schedule Workouts with Your Board Members

Having a gym partner who also happens to be someone you work with can have its benefits. This will allow you to not only maintain a schedule, but help you build a deeper relationship with the student leader.

Plan Meals Weekly or Bi-Weekly with Others

Meals are an opportunity to "be social" and "catch up" with friends. There would be weeks where I would be swamped with school, work, and office duties. I was unable to spend as much time with my friends as I would have liked. Planning dinner dates, meetings for lunch, or even a cup of coffee were perfect ways for me to grab a meal, and spend time with others. I would also plan meetings over meals with administrators, mentors, and counselors. It was a double bonus to not only get out of the office, but a great way to hear some new concerns, and even suggestions from leaders all across campus. When I was not meeting with officials during my lunch, I would be eating outside or with my constituents. The more you are seen in public, even during lunch time, the better.

Consider a Sleep Schedule

No matter how odd, strange, or nonexistent you think

your sleep cycle is, at least consider sticking to it. Although I highly recommend getting as much sleep as possible, there is something to be said for maintaining a set cycle that works both for your schedule as a student leader, and for your body. If you find yourself operating on 4-5 hours of sleep a night, experiment for a week and try a 20-minute nap in the middle of the day. No time for one? See what activities you can cut from your schedule or improve its efficiency. Try new ways of managing your time and see what works for you. From my personal experience not sleeping well goes hand in and with procrastination. As long as you are on schedule and on time with your deliverables, your chances of getting some sleep will improve drastically.

During my time in office I coordinated office hours with some members of my team to do homework together. We would sit, talk, laugh, finish what we needed to do for class, and grab dinner and drinks to celebrate our productivity after. Take care of your health, get sleep, eat real meals, and enjoy the ride! Do not forget to keep in mind that your body will last with you long after your term, hopefully, so take care of it. Learn to leverage your position and the doors it opens to launch you into the future you want to create for yourself. Ask questions, seek out mentors, and put yourself out there. During my time in office, I invited one faculty, staff member, or student leader on campus out for coffee once a week. It not only led to invaluable insights into what issues were pertinent on campus and to whom, but it also expanded my perspective, networks, and what I saw as possible throughout my term. To this day, those networks and relationships play an invaluable role in my life, and they can for you too.

Constituent based advocacy

As a student representing students, how do you keep your head about you when it comes to working with administration, faculty, staff, and your constituents? This may be the most challenging responsibility you face, but it is not impossible. During my term, there were five questions I asked myself before making any choices when I felt torn between the expectations of my constituents, the administration, and even of my own. Try them and see where it leads you:

- What is the need I am addressing?
- Who does this choice concern and who does this choice affect?
- Why is this issue important (to my constituents and to the University)?
- What is the impact of my choice and where will it lead?
- What is my role and who do I serve?

When in a leadership position, it can be easy to get caught up in the glitz and glory of a title. But the title means nothing if you do not exercise the power behind it for the betterment and empowerment of those around you. As a student advocate you have to be selfless in your position. Again, this is not about you. This is about identifying the needs of a community and stepping up to the plate with confidence and humility and fulfilling those needs on behalf of your constituents.

Being a Servant

When you think of the word servant, what are the first things that come to mind? If you are anything like me when I first took the time to think of the word, I thought of people - maids, butlers, and drivers, someone who did things for other people. I foolishly thought the word described someone weak. Subservient. It was not until my senior year in college when I actually understood what servant actually means - someone who enables others to become more. Now when I think about the word servant, I think about power. It is not a person at all, let alone a weak one; and bears not even the slightest similarity to someone who is powerless. Rather, a servant empowers those they serve to grow. Servant leadership allows others to become servants themselves. To keep yourself and your team in check, ask yourself: do your actions as a servant leader inspire others to be of service too? Does the bill you pass move your community to act as well? Empowering others to become more and do more through your service - that is the true mark of leadership.

Being a Leader

Any leadership position can be a roller coaster ride of unexpected events, incredible victories, frustrating standstills, and unbelievable progress. Prior to taking office, you should have already created for yourself a platform, list, or set of objectives you are setting out to tackle and accomplish during your term. These points are your guiding light throughout your term. These are the tangible, realistic, attainable goals, commitments, and promises that you must keep in mind.

Relish every victory your team has fought for and remember there is always another game to play tomorrow. Learn from your upsets and what led you there, yet stay motivated and hungry for the bigger vision you have in mind.

Keep yourself and your team grounded. Leading a group of leaders can be a challenge overcome by accountability, communication, and support. Each person is different, and each person's needs are different as well. One way my cabinet and I addressed this was conducting three weeks' worth of individual one-on-ones with every member of our organization. We asked questions like: How do you work under stress? What are your goals for this year? What are ways we can support you? What is your favorite go-to drink at Starbucks? By getting to know your team, it helps you to know how they operate. Just as you are a student, advocate, servant, and a leader, remember, they are too.

Staying Grounded
Those you choose to surround yourself with are not only

a direct reflection of who you are, but also feed you an energy that will affect your work and results. Be accountable to one another and lean on each other for support. In my experience, my team reminded me after a disappointment or loss to remember the bigger picture we were fighting for, just as many times as they reminded me to celebrate a victory. You are each other's anchors whether you believe it or not, and each of your victories belongs to you as a group.

What I mean by "staying grounded" is to be present, be humble, and be genuine. Do not get lost in the power your position can hold, and simultaneously, do not take for granted the privilege others have given you. Do not play this game like you are the expert and you are here to teach everyone how to play - everyone is learning, and everyone is growing. Some of my best moments in office were times when I learned how to listen and follow just as much as I developed the skills to speak and lead. So enjoy yourself and do not take yourself too seriously. Whether you are passing an exam, conducting a meeting, considering how to best serve your constituents, or leading your peers, be present in the situation that is before you. The most powerful people are connected to reality. It can be difficult to balance, but the very fact that you are reading this book, already means you are one step closer to attaining it. Trust your gut, after all it has gotten you this far.

KEY CONCEPTS

1. In your position you actually have four roles: student, advocate, servant, and leader.

2. You are a student representing students. Knowing this, you have a responsibility not only to your constituents, but also to yourself, to carry out your academic career with as much passion as you would your office.

3. Maintaining sleep, a healthy diet, and exercise are important to your success as a student leader.

4. The title means nothing if you do not exercise the power behind it for the betterment and empowerment of those around you.

5. Consider being a student leader a game. Do not act like you are the expert- everyone is learning, everyone is growing.

MY REFLECTION

MARIAM SALAMEH | FORMER STUDENT BODY PRESIDENT
CALIFORNIA STATE UNIVERSITY, STANISLAUS

As a former ASI President, I have learned that a leader who leads must be humble and selfless. Having a title can sometimes ruin a person's self-identity through the process of developing yourself as a leader. You need to remember to be true to yourself and to those that you represent. In my two terms in office, I have faced adversity and challenges that have molded me into the leader, professional, and person I am today. Staying grounded has guided me to not lose focus on my goals and accomplishments. I have learned to surround myself with leaders and mentors that challenged, inspired, and motivated me every day. These individuals held me accountable and continuously reminded me of the bigger picture, which was to represent the students' voice.

The best advice that I can give to upcoming leaders is to have a great support system that will remind and hold you accountable to your words and actions. My ASI family was one of my greatest support system that kept me on the right track. If there was a time that I was not on the right track, they would be the first to communicate to me on ways to improve and reprioritize. Having an open door policy really helped me to have those honest and at times candid conversations with people whom I had the privilege to work with.

The power of the title can stir you away from your goals and accomplishments. As a leader, you can easily lose track and focus when you are pulled in every direction with projects and commitments. However, just remember to breathe and reprioritize and always remember those that elected you, those who believe in you, and the greater mission to leave a positive impact.

15. ORGANIZATIONAL CONTINUITY
ROHULLAH LATIF | STUDENT BODY PRESIDENT
CALIFORNIA STATE UNIVERSITY, FULLERTON

Something about student leadership sparked your interest, so you took the next step, researched, applied, and were appointed/elected to a leadership position. You gave it all you had and now you are terming out. You feel great about your accomplishments and everyone is impressed with your work. You still have a few more weeks and your successor just got elected/appointed. Now what? Now it's time to continue your legacy! What good is building a house if there is no one to maintain it? It is crucial for leaders to pass down their knowledge onto the next generations. After all that is how organizations continue to thrive. So how do you update an incoming student leader with a year's worth of information through only a few weeks of succession planning?

Succession planning is utilizing the resources of your organization to train, develop, and mentor the next generation of leaders in whatever role they've been elected or appointed to. Why is it important? Earlier, we mentioned that "student leadership positions are temporary" because student leaders graduate, find a job, or develop other interests and move on. Student governments are complex organizations that have so many moving parts internally and face an ever evolving world externally. Combine that with the fact that many of these organizations have a limited amount of institutional knowledge and you have a recipe for failure if a student is not properly matriculated through the ins and outs of student leadership. Some students thrive in a sink or swim environment, others need some guidance, and some are a mixture of both. Regardless of where you fall in that continuum, understand that some form of succession planning is necessary for your success as a leader and the continuation of your organization.

Legacy Binder/Files

Planning for a successful transition starts on your first day in office. It is important to record all of your meetings, agendas, notes, and projects early on rather than scrambling towards the end to put everything together.

Start off with a large 3 ring binder and add multiple tabs with labels. The first tab should be a letter from you to the next leader. You can do this towards the end and make sure you add a photo of yourself and a quick bio. The next few tabs should be dedicated to your projects. State if you were successful, if not why? Include a tab with clippings from newspapers and any other media coverage you received during your term. Since history sometime repeats itself, it is critical that you make note of events that took place, like student fee increases or student or faculty strikes. Be sure to explain the reason for each event and how you and your team handled it. Include a tab dedicated to all the lessons you've learned about the position over your term. Your interactions with administrators, staff, faculty, and students should also be included. With a yearly turnover rate, student government policies and documents tend to change as the leadership changes. For this reason, add a tab in the binder for position descriptions and copies of all important documents such as constitutions, policies, and procedures. Budgets from prior years and financial documents are important information to pass down, especially if there were major budget cuts or increases. Providing templates for forms, letters, minutes, agendas, and Robert's Rules of Order can also help new leaders with running meetings. Lastly, dedicate the final tab for contact information. Using a spreadsheet, tally up all the important contacts you feel the next person should meet or know. These could range from student clubs and organizations to administrators and notable alumni's. These are some of the many topics you can cover in your binder. If you feel like saving some trees, you can also have this folder saved on a shared drive or on a cloud file.

Experienced vs Inexperienced

More often than not, you will have someone appointed or elected who has very limited experience. I have personally seen this happen multiple times. This becomes especially difficult when the person you were supporting is not chosen to take your position. Nevertheless, you still have one last responsibility and that is to put aside your feelings and help with the transition. If not for the betterment of the organization, then do it for the student body.

Ultimately, the new administration's success or failure will impact your students. Do not let your personal bias get in the way of educating the next leaders, even if they are your mortal enemy. If the person already has previous experience, great! It will make your job much easier. If they are not experienced, take the time to start ASAP! If they were appointed or elected on a Friday, set up a transition for the following week and start the transition process. You will have to handle each student leader differently. Someone who is experienced and someone who is inexperienced will bring different skills to the table and you will have to tailor your transition to them.

Transition process

Once your successor has been identified, the ball is in your court. Immediately set up a meeting with them and if applicable, with their team. I recommend this meeting to be informal. Get to know the individual and share a cup of coffee. Sometimes the best meetings do not take place in an office or a building. This is an opportunity to build cohesiveness amongst two different generations of leaders. Some organizations will provide funds to have a transition retreat, if not, see if you could arrange one. Utilize your resources to the best of your ability. During the transition meeting, go over your entire legacy binder. Do not just show them what you've done, ask them questions and get their feedback. See what they've would have done differently. This will allow them to get a taste of the obstacles they might face early on. Provide them opportunities to shadow you by bringing them to meetings, introducing them to key players on campus, and overall just get them used to your busy schedule. If time is not on your side an e-introduction to various campus administrators, club and the organization's leaders, and faculty members is appropriate. Usually, newly elected student leaders are not fully aware of how much work these positions require, so it's important to prepare them in advance.

All of this information could be too much to take in a short period of time. For this reason, be patient and encourage them to ask questions. Offer your assistance and if you feel comfortable enough, offer these individuals your contact information, but be prepared for the random email at 1:00 am in the event they need assistance. What if they do not agree or share the same vision as you? Or worse, what if they refuse to participate and work with you altogether? The answer is simple, be the bigger person and still offer a transition meeting. If you can, try to announce this meeting in some public setting. It helps people remember that you are still in the game and are still taking the initiative to help your organization.

Move on

Like the movie Frozen put it, "let it go." Many student leaders who had it good for the few years in leadership roles grow overly attached to the positions. Even after graduation, they will try to exercise their powers and constantly share their viewpoints in person or on social media. Please do not be that person! There is nothing wrong about helping as an alumnus of that position, but do not overdo it. You have graduated, move on to bigger leadership roles.

Alumni Engagement

While you are still in office you can help bridge the gap between your organization and the alumni organization. This helps with organizational continuity by having a system in place to constantly keep in contact with student leaders who graduate. Staying in touch with alumni who were student leaders only strengthens the transition process. More than just the ability to provide financial resources, alumni can also help provide career and internship opportunities for your constituents. They can also help provide institutional knowledge that you may not be aware of and help you develop relationships with people on campus and the community.

Early on during your term, develop a relationship with your alumni board on campus. This will allow you to tap into their database and locate certain alumni's that could help you with your initiative. Once you have located your alumni, there are various ways to provide them with information or get them reconnected and involved.

Alumni Night

This can be a great way to get alumni in one place and showcase what you and your administration have been able to accomplish. It can also show that you are appreciative of their support in whatever capacity. This event could also be a chance to have a scholarship fundraiser.

Alumni of the Month/Where are they now?

Selecting a certain alumni and shining a spotlight on them can be great for alumni engagement. Some universities have an "alumni of the month" or a "where are they now?"

Newsletters

A newsletter is a great way to share what your organization has been doing. This can not only be communicated to students, administrators, and the community, but also alumni of your organization. We recommend a quarterly or biannual newsletter because a monthly one is tedious and not necessary.

After I gave that speech in front of 1000's of people, I began to reminisce of all the good times. Remember to cherish every moment of your time as a student leader. A lot of people ask me, "don't you miss being the President, the big shot on campus?" My answer is simply no, I do not. I do not miss it because I gave it all I had during my term.

I left no room for regret and you should not either. The skills you acquire as a student leader will set you apart from all of your colleagues. I learned early on, that my position and this feeling of power is temporary. The real world will not be the same, but I am prepared to face it head on, just as my successor will have to face their new position.

KEY CONCEPTS

1. Succession planning is utilizing the resources of your organization to train, develop, and mentor the next generation of leaders in whatever role to which they have been elected or appointed.

2. It is important to record all of your meetings, agendas, notes, and projects early on rather than scrambling towards the end to put everything together.

3. Once your successor has been identified, the ball is in your court. Immediately set up a meeting with them and if applicable, with their team. I recommend this meeting to be informal.

4. You have graduated, move on to bigger leadership roles.

MY REFLECTION

TALAR ALEXANIAN | FORMER STUDENT TRUSTEE
BOARD OF TRUSTEES, CALIFORNIA STATE UNIVERSITY

After years of student leadership at Cal State Northridge and as a Trustee of the 23 California State University campuses, I've learned a thing or two about student leadership. However, one very important lesson is that every organization you're affiliated with has its own brand. And as a student leader, you represent that brand. The way brands succeed, achieve name recognition, and have the power to truly create an impact is through organizational continuity. On the job, I would always wonder what the future of my organizations would be like after I graduated and moved on to my post college life out in the "real world." That's why I used every opportunity during my leadership to put systems & structures in place that would succeed me long after I'm gone.

This ensures the transfer of institutional knowledge from one set of leaders to the next and maintains and expands the organization's relationships with key partners and stakeholders. For example, during my term as student body Vice President, we noticed that students were concerned with two overarching issues. One was the desire to build a strong sense of campus community and the other was the lack of available healthy food options. And so, we created the first ever CSUN Farmer's Market to fulfill this need.

It may sound easy, but it took a lot of energy, research, patience, relationship building, collaboration, and negotiation with our university partners to make our vision a reality.

As a result, students, faculty, and staff alike now had access to healthier options on campus that catered to the preferences of those who are gluten-free, vegan and vegetarian. The weekly market also fostered that sense of community we were looking. Every Tuesday, everyone knew where to go and shop for groceries, enjoy live music, and connect with friends, both old and new. After its success, we created a resolution announcing the market's launch and codified student government's commitment to fund the market for a minimum of three years. What good is creating an event with such a large scale impact if you cannot see it grow and impact future students?

When you come up with a new idea, an innovative program, or find a different way of getting things done, it's important to focus on its longevity just as much as its success during your short term. Since graduation, I've been there as a mentor for my successors and their team. I've been invited as a recent alumna to share leadership lessons I've learned to the 5,000 new freshmen looking to begin their journey of campus involvement. Now I've certainly missed my positions and my ability to lead key initiatives on both the campus and statewide level, but I remind myself of the changes I was able to implement and the impact I did make during my term. It's time for someone with a new vision to take on the reigns and build on the foundation already in place. As for me, it's time to tackle a new adventure armed with the skills student leadership passed on to me.

EPILOGUE

This book is dedicated to student leaders who have advanced the student agenda in a way that ensured that student voices were heard. Those who will never receive any form of recognition. Those whose names will never be engraved anywhere. Those whose names will be forgotten as soon as they step off campus. This book is dedicated to the nameless student who stayed up late at the office preparing the next morning's agenda or slept in their office working on a project for the campus. This book is dedicated to you.

When the authors came together we had one idea in mind, we wanted to ensure that the next generation had what we never had. We wanted to highlight the efforts put in by every student leader so they may be immortalized in some capacity. In your hands, you hold the collective knowledge of several student government leaders. The authors ask one thing: use this knowledge for good.

Go further than we ever thought possible. Do what we only dreamed of doing. Use what you have gained from this book to make the collegiate setting a better place. Do so with the understanding that you may become that nameless student, but that is what student government is: A Selfless Service.

UNIVERSITIES REPRESENTED
(NATIONALLY AND INTERNATIONALLY)

California State University, Channel Islands (Camarillo)
California State University, Chico
California State University, Fresno
California State University, Fullerton
California State University, Long beach
California State University, Northridge
San Jose State University
California State University, Stanislaus
Citrus Community College
Cork Institute of Technology, Ireland
Fresno City Community College
Santa Clara University
The Johns Hopkins University
University of California Davis
University of California Riverside
University of Massachusetts Amherst
University of Notre Dame
University of the Pacific

MAJORS

Mechanical Engineering, Biomedical Engineering, Student Affairs, Pre-Law, Business, Communication, Political Science, Law, Sustainable Agriculture and Environmental Policy, Higher Education Administration, Business Administration, Public Administration, Sociology, Marketing, Media Relations

Made in the USA
San Bernardino,
CA